MALTA

Mosta ●

Sliema ●

a ●

VALLETTA ●
Senglea ●

Luqa ●

Marsascala ●

Marsaxlokk ●

Ħaġar Qim ●

Birżebbuġa ●

UNCOMMON

MALTA & GOZO

Emma Mattei & Jon Banthorpe

MIRANDA

First published in Malta 2011

Published by
Miranda Publishers
139/3 Tower Road,
Sliema, Malta.
www.mirandabooks.com

ISBN 9789990985504

Designed by Jon Banthorpe
www.reasonsfor.com

Printed in Malta by
Progress Press

The opinions expressed in this book are those of the authors etc.
Facts are deemed correct at time of going to print,
some may be subject
to change.

Edited by Emma Mattei

www.uncommonguidebooks.com

It is not down in any map: true places never are.

Herman Melville

INDEX

Għajn Tuffieħa

FOREWORD

Malta has been a crossroads and a haven for as long as man has travelled across the Mediterranean Sea, and all those who have come this way have left their mark. An island nation with a history dating back to 3600 BC, this archipelago lies between the coast of Tunisia and the southernmost tip of Sicily, and gives testament to the region's intricate maritime histories.

When faced with the question - who are the Maltese? - it is tempting to provide an abbreviated timeline across centuries and civilisations, hoping to open a window onto Maltese identity: the Temple Period; the Bronze Age; the Phoenicians; the Greeks; the Carthaginians; the Romans; the Arabs; the Normans; the Spanish; the many-langued Knights of the Order of Saint John; the French; the British and independence in 1964.

Open any guide book and it will attempt to précis Malta's history in this manner, before providing all the necessary information on where to stay, where to visit, where to be entertained and how to get there.

It might be more telling, however, to point out that contemporary Malta, is at once both outward looking, yet steadfastly resilient. It is a nation that looks fiercely to its past and clings to its cultural pillars, whilst seeking modernity, architectural reinvention, social liberation and rapid economic growth. It is a heady cocktail of tradition, politics, religion and the dream of a comfortable home, all under a bright sun.

Uncommon is a companion and travelogue that provides multiple avenues to unravel some of the complexities that may overwhelm and disorient the unfamiliar, and to reveal the many layers that make up the public and private spheres. There are four sections in the book: *Relate, Review, Recreate* and *Reroute*, each providing a way to connect with the inhabitants, the streets, the buildings and quotidian life.

Uncommon is made up of subjective explorations of the country's history, diversity and lore. In it you will find contemporary reportage, travel writing and historical anecdote, curiosa and customs revealed and reinterpreted, memory maps, off-beat routes, itineraries and aimless meanderings taken in the spirit of Guy Debord's dérive. The stories and suggestions are provided by a wide-ranging group of contributors: Maltese living here and abroad, expatriates who are resident and visitors, both frequent and novel.

Uncommon is the field manual for the contemporary explorer; the authors invite you to engage with the islands in a novel and intimate way, and hope you will also leave your mark just as many have done before.

Emma Mattei & Jon Banthorpe

RELATE

NOVEL TALES & INTIMATE HISTORIES FROM THE URBAN SPRAWL

A TRIP TO 18th CENTURY VALLETTA

Liam Gauci

Forget cheap flights, forget a nice hotel room, we will be travelling back in time. Around 200 years to be precise, for a trip to Malta in the 18th century. A time when Malta was home to the Knights of St. John. The last crusaders of Europe. The Knights of St. John were noble men who had devoted their life to caring for the sick, protecting the poor and defending Europe. To achieve this they had taken vows of obedience, chastity and poverty. This Order had transformed Malta into a small principality, unlike anything in the Mediterranean.

Nature had given Malta the best laid-out blue print for a harbour, and then all the Knights had to do was to fit into the jigsaw the missing pieces. Malta was transformed from a barren rock into a small state in the Mediterranean. The rising bastions fitted in perfectly with the white sandstone of Malta; the clustered, flat-roofed pumpkin-coloured houses of Valletta, Floriana, and the Three Cities floated in the centre of the Mediterranean Sea. Valletta had become the impregnable city about which Louis XIV had once said that no army, however large, would ever hope to overrun.

The knights had constructed and adapted one of the largest harbours in Europe into one of the safest havens in the Mediterranean. Sailors, Merchants, Actors, Musicians, Chocolate Makers, Poets, Treasure Hunters, Prostitutes, Gamblers and Thieves were attracted to this island state. The Knights were a mixed company of expert sailors, good administrators, philanders and loafers. Many were bored, most were rich, on the whole they were brave; the greatest legend of Christendom found active expression in an order at once monastic and chivalrous. And these are the people who we would have met in 18th century Valletta.

To travel to Malta one had to make his way to Southern Italy, then travel southwards through Sicily until you arrived in Syracuse were you could hail a Maltese Speronara, a swift boat which was the safest way to the island of Malta. One traveller, Patrick Brydone, gives us his take on his voyage arrangements to Malta in the 1770s. He had just boarded a Maltese Speronara, and he and a couple of friends were making their way by boat to Capo Passero, the southernmost part of Sicily. As night was closing he writes:

"….we have likewise made an admirable and a very comfortable disposition

3

for our night's lodging. The Speronara is so very narrow, that it is impossible for us all to lie in it, besides, we are eaten up with vermin, and have nothing but hard boards to lie in on. All these considerations, added to the cursed swinging of the boat and the horrid sickness it occasions, have determined us rather to trust ourselves to the mercy of the *banditi*, than to lie another night at sea…a great quantity of fine, soft, dry sea weed lying under the shelter of a rock, seems intended by providence for our bed, over this we are going to stretch a sail and expect to sleep most luxuriously"

This detail from Patrick Brydone's diary gives us a clue to what tourists travelling to Malta went through; when they finally made their crossing over they usually travelled by night as to avoid any pirates roaming the seas, Brydone further on writes about his experience of the Sicily-Malta crossing:

" a little after nine we embarked. The night was delightfull, the wind had died away, and we were obliged to ply our oars….the coast of Sicily began to recede and in a short time we found ourselves in the ocean. There was a profound silence, except the noise of the waves breaking on the distant shore, which only served to render the scene more solemn. The moon shone bright on the water… the scene had naturally sunk us into meditation, we had remained near an hour without speaking a word when our sailors (Maltese) began their midnight hymn to the Virgin. The music was simple, solemn, and in perfect harmony with the scene and with all our feelings. They beat exact time with their oars, and observed the harmony with the utmost perfection. We listened with infinite pleasure to this melancholy concert, and felt the vanity of operas and oratorios were feeble compared to such moments…at last they sung us asleep…we were now on the ocean…"

To arrive in Malta took around 8 to 12 hours of sailing, once you approached the Grand Harbour you would here the roar of the saluting guns from the bastions of Valletta. Once inside the harbour you had to present a clean bill of health, giving proof that whence you had left, the plague was not raging. If all was well you would disembark and walk into Valletta. With the yellow Maltese stone shining in the morning sun, you could then start to admire your new holiday destination. Brydone did just that:

"on getting on shore, we found ourselves in a new world indeed. The streets crowded with well dressed people, who have all the appearance of health and affluence, whereas at Syracuse, there was scarce a creature to be seen, and even those few had the appearance of disease and wretchedness"

The next thing a traveller had to do was to look for the nearest tavern. These taverns could provide you with a warm meal and a nice, clean bed for the night. Being still morning, once you had unloaded your baggage, you could order a warm cup of the local coffee to kick start your day. Malta was renowned for its coffee. The Maltese recipe for it was a mixture of coffee, cloves and sugar. Coffee had originated in Ethiopia and was an Ottoman indulgence. The church in Malta frowned upon this "Devil's" drink. But within a few years everyone loved it and the drink became a favourite on the island. In 1665 Domenico Magri, a Maltese doctor, wrote about how coffee drove away sexual desires, reduced stomach cramps and kept university students awake throughout the night.

Anybody who visited Malta was bound to admire the beauty of Valletta; built by Grand Master La Valette on a grid-like pattern, the buildings rose in 'monastic block-like buildings'. The city had to bear the virtue of monastic simplicity, but by the eighteenth century, the hardened warriors tempted themselves and kept with the European ideal of the time to show grandeur in their buildings. Walking through the streets even today one can admire the beauty of the architecture. Valletta of the Knights had been converted into a jewel of a city, crowned by the most beautiful of diamonds in the shape of the conventual church of St. John (the co-cathedral). Originally it was a simple, elegant church as befitted a religious order, but gradually it was transformed into a mausoleum for the finest of European chivalry. Decoration in this church is as unnatural as the sweetness of a wedding cake. By the end of the seventeenth century not an inch of space was bare from decoration. Everywhere the eight-tongued cross of the Hospitallers: breastplates, helmets, double-headed eagles, trophies, and ornate cannons filled this mausoleum for the Knights.

Another beautiful building which one could visit in Valletta during the 18th century and still existing today was the palace of the grandmaster. If you were lucky enough, you could admire the Grandmaster in his daily routine of conversations with the local ladies, gossiping away, sipping hot chocolate and eating sweet pastries. The Grandmaster kept up this daily routine and always agreed with their lamentations against their husbands. He poured the hot chocolate for these ladies from specially- made silver chocolate pots. Hot chocolate was a favourite hot drink in Malta and it was drunk by everybody. The grand master himself had his own chocolatier. On board the ships of the Order, chocolate was served to everybody; even the slaves, who rowed the galleys were served chocolate every evening. Sweets were also enjoyed in Malta. One of the oldest recipe books found at the Biblioteca in Valletta dates back to 1748. It was written by Michele Mercieca, and holds within its hand written pages recipes for biscuits, chocolate mousse, as well as ice creams.

Ice creams were all the rage in Malta and these were prepared with the weirdest of ingredients including, parmesan, and pistachio. Nonetheless, chocolate ice cream remained the most sought after flavour. Napoleon himself was offered ice cream when he conquered Malta in 1798, but apparently the young conqueror was not interested in tasting the specially prepared ice creams. Ice cream in Malta was prepared in cylindrical containers, whereby ice from Mount Etna was mixed with the chocolate, coffee, lemons or whatever the recipe required. Special boats brought this ice on a daily basis to Malta, and kept the knights and their subjects well supplied with this cool thirst quencher in the hot climate of Malta.

All this travelling round Valletta would have made tourists hungry. A spot of lunch at a local tavern would have been perfect. Some macaroni and cheese or some vermicelli with bottarga would have been a popular snack served in Malta. The latter was very popular in taverns, especially during lent. Vermicelli, that is long, thin, spaghetti, was boiled and then tossed in olive oil, garlic and parsley, after which bottarga was grated over the dish. Bottarga was produced in Sicily and Sardinia where tuna roe was dried, salted, moulded into sausage shapes and exported to Malta, where it was eaten by all of society.

After lunch a brisk walk to the Upper Barrakka gardens could be on the cards. Here one could admire the view of the harbour as well as sip on some orange or cinnamon liqueur. Liqueurs, as well as oranges, were very sought after in Malta.

Maltese oranges were popular all over the world. In fact if one was lucky enough one would be able to visit the tract of land the daughters of Louis XV of France had rented out in Malta especially to grow Maltese oranges. These oranges were enjoyed for their sweetness and fragrant smells. As Patrick Brydone remarked: "The juice of this fruit is red as blood, and of a fine flavour. The greatest part of their crop is sent in presents to the different courts of Europe, and the relations of the chevaliers. It was not without a good deal of difficulty that we procured a few chests for our friends in Naples."

A look at the harbour from atop the bastions would give you a clear view of the Grand Harbour. Fleets of various nations, British, French, Russian and Spanish navies were always calling at Malta. This gave the surrounding cities a cosmopolitan feel. The most notorious frequenters of the harbour were the Maltese corsairs. The toughest and roughest sailors in the Mediterranean. Becoming a corsair was not easy, but it was a great career. You would apply for a license from the Grand Master (the prince of Malta), swear to provide him with 10% of your profits, and he would give you permission to fit out a corsair ship. A captain then found sponsors, Knights, merchants, rich noblemen, even wealthy women, who would provide the money injection to procure a ship, weapons, cannons and sailors. On board these ships you would find people from various parts of the world, Austrians, Englishmen, Greeks, Spaniards, Russians and Maltese serving under one flag, that of the Order of St. John. A career in corsairing was a real chance for anybody, from whatever background, to really have a go at becoming rich.

And if at the end of your day you would visit a local tavern you would easily have met one of these corsairs drinking Aqua Vitae (grappa) mixed with black powder, and 'investing' in women of ill repute. Captain Alonso De Contreras was one such corsair. He became obsessed with a local wench, as he chose to call her, and gave her so much money that she started investing in real estate in Valletta. Until one fine day he came back from a corsairing expedition and found her in bed with another man. In a fuming rage he ran her lover through with his sword and chased the terrified woman all the way to Sicily.

Valletta in the evening must have been a city teeming with activity; taverns serving wine, rum and grappa, musicians playing and woman of ill repute round every corner. Various travellers described the harbour as the Tavern of Europe. The local women were described by a Polish traveller thus: "The fair sex is very fair in Malta, their principal attractions being a waist of extremely svelte, a leg beautifully formed, an instep finely arched, a skin of dazzling whiteness, a bust of splendid proportions, hair as black as ebony..."

If merry making in the taverns was not for you then you could choose to visit the Manoel Theatre, where various performances were held. The theatre was constructed to provide honest entertainment for the public of Malta. It proved to be very popular, but the pious inquisitor got worried about the number of young knights who were getting involved in the theatre and taking on female roles.

After an evening out, dinner was always a good time to indulge in some good local cuisine, rabbit fried in wine, garlic and onions. Or some ravioli filled with local goat's cheese, or maybe even some oxtail soup. Whatever your choice, a filling dinner would get you ready for bed at your taverna. Therefore, before

Costume – Valetta.

A street in Valletta. A watercolour from a diary at the Malta Maritime Museum

we leave 18th century Valletta, whenever you wrap your hand around a cup of coffee or taste some home made ravioli in Malta always spare a thought for the past travellers and inhabitants of the island!

We will leave 18th century Malta with another extract from Patrick Brydone diary:

"Mr. Rutter immediately conducted us to an inn which had more the appearance of a palace. We have had an excellent supper, and good burgundy; and as this is the king's birthday, we have almost got tipsy to his health.

We are now going into clean, comfortable beds, in expectations of the sweetest slumbers....Good night. I would not lose a moment of it for the world. People may say what they please but there is no enjoyment in living in perpetual ease and affluence, and true luxury is only to be attained by undergoing a few hardships. But this is no time to philosophise. So Adieu."

ON THE FLOOR

Bettina Hutschek

"I am looking for creatures," I tell the man who is watching me suspiciously. My hands clean away hair and dust – I am on my knees. It is no religious activity which has lead me to inch around the St John's co-cathedral floor for the past two weeks, it is these wild creations; underneath the thick, plastic carpets, wolves are roaming the marble, eagles and lions are everywhere and even an astronaut is waving his antennae. A book of imaginary beings comes to life under my feet: nameless hybrids and mythical beasts pop up from the floor. I see pygmies, dragons, jellyfish, cockroaches, angels, nymphs, a rabbit (the Lunar Hare) and a unicorn. I see weapons, warships, fire and skeletons. A yellow ox trots along black fields. A phoenix snares at ordinary birds. A winged hourglass tries to fly out of Father Time's hands; the clocks are broken. It is as if all those skulls and bones had brought along another world, a magical timeless world of fantastical creatures for us to look at, not as a reminder of death and decay, but as a reminder of life. I start talking to them, and they tell their stories. Lady goose has an idea; a shooting star comes out of her head. Dancing angels blaspheme at the Lamia - half woman, half serpent - who whistle sweetly since they cannot speak. Less gentle are the Harpies, with women's faces and vultures' bodies, eternally stuck in their insatiable hunger and their foul smell. Putti lovingly cradle skulls, while an Indian is studying Roman numbers. A griffin comments on my nail polish. I am laughing to myself as towers collapse. The Cheshire Cat joins my laughter. We step on beauty.

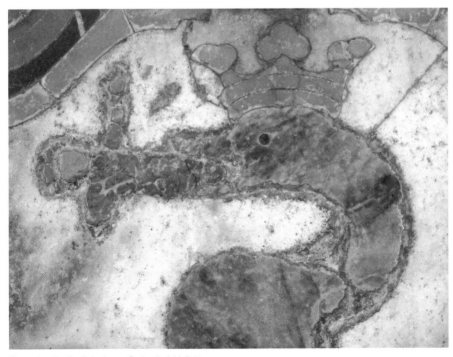

Floor details, St. John's co-Cathedral, Valletta

BYRON'S ENCOUNTER WITH 'CALYPSO'

Peter Vassallo

When the *Townsend* packet dropped anchor in the Grand Harbour at Malta, at noon on the 31st August 1809, two of its passengers remained on deck apparently waiting for a welcoming salvo from the saluting battery. One of them Lord Byron, a handsome aristocrat, author of the satire English Bards, was visibly annoyed when the guns remained silent. He was then aged twenty-three, the sixth Baron Byron of Rochdale and a member of the House of Lords, and was expecting the customary welcome given to an important visitor which he felt was his due. The other, his staunchly loyal Cambridge friend ('his bulldog') John Cam Hobhouse (later to become Lord Broughton), was accompanying the poet on his Mediterranean tour and they were stopping in Malta en route to the Orient.

Disappointed, they both cleared customs and trudged up the 'nix mangiare' steps bristling with importunate beggars, past the drawbridge near Ġnien Is-Sultan leading into Valletta and then slowly climbed the stairs where they eventually found lodgings at the top of Old Bakery Street, then known as Strada di Forni. The climb was painful and it exhausted Byron who felt the pressure on his lame right foot of those 'cursed streets of stairs'. The Casa di San Poix where they had taken lodgings was a spacious mansion originally belonging to the Bali of the Order of St. John, the very house where Coleridge had stayed for a while during his Malta sojourn earlier in 1804-5.

A few days later Byron and Hobhouse were invited to a reception at the house of a Mrs. Fraser, wife of Commander Fraser, who had literary ambitions and who had composed a poem Camilla de Florian which she eager to show Byron. During the reception Byron was introduced to Mrs. Fraser's constant companion, a certain Mrs. Spencer Smith, an attractive woman, who though only four years older than the poet, had led a remarkably adventurous and romantic life. Constance Spencer Smith was actually the daughter of Baron Herbert, the Austrian Ambassador to Constantinople, who had been imprisoned in Italy under direct orders from Napoleon, but rescued in most romantic fashion by her daring admirer, the gallant Marquis de Salvo who had used a ladder, rope and disguise and horses in what we now call true Hollywood style. Her husband was the British Ambassador to Stuttgart and happened to be abroad at the time. Byron was fascinated by this beautiful adventuress (this 'contemporary Calypso' who had enchanted him) and was consequently in no hurry to proceed on his travels with Hobhouse. He gave her his emerald ring as a gift and token of his admiration and was secretly planning to sail to Friuli with her. Matters came to a head when a certain Captain Carey, aide de camp to the Civil High Commissioner Major General Hildebrand Oakes, made some snide remarks at dinner presumably directed at Byron's liaison with Constance Spencer Smith and he further annoyed the poet by grinning knowingly. In a moment of rashness Byron sent the grinning Captain a brief letter challenging him to a duel 'on account of the insolence of your behaviour' adding that his remarks about him were 'not to be tolerated'. The duel was fixed for six in the morning of the 8th September outside the gates of Floriana, known as the 'Bombes'. Hobhouse, alarmed at his friend's rashness and the imminent danger he had placed himself in (for Captain Carey was an expert shot), went over to the Captain's adjutant, Captain Waddle, at midnight, in a desperate attempt to settle the matter honourably. Hobhouse managed to obtain a sort of muted apology and Byron for his part was to give his word as a gentleman that he would observe the 'strictest secrecy' about this affair. The 'warlike' Captain eventually agreed and this awkward matter was settled. Hobhouse saw to it that they both boarded the first ship bound for Albania and Byron was tactfully whisked out of harm's way, but not before making a lover's tryst with Constance that they should meet again and renew their liaison in Malta after a year and a day. Some months later Byron conceived the idea of writing a verse account of his travels which he entitled Childe Harold's Pilgrimage, a narrative poem in Spenserian stanzas, which was to bring him instant fame and in which he projected himself as a latter-day Odysseus drifting perilously in the Mediterranean. He also portrayed Constance as a 'new Calypso' lying in wait (on Calypso's isle) ready to ensnare poets like himself with her irresistible beauty. But, of course, the hero is Byronic, not Homeric, and is, in the poem, projected as a blasé and cynical man of the world who remains impervious to the snares of love and the glitter of a beautiful woman's eyes.

Calypso, also referred to as 'Fair Florence' in the poem, kept to her side of the bargain and duly returned to Malta a year later but was intensely disappointed not to find the poet there. But Byron dallied in Greece and Albania as the magical period of his infatuation, 'his ambrosial amour', gradually wore off.

On his returned to Calypso's isle, almost a year later, he was compelled to undergo quarantine and, almost bored out of his mind, he wrote a few dismal reflections on the state of his physical and mental health. Out of sheer boredom he carved his name on the inner courtyard of the Lazaretto where he was confined for two weeks.

After performing quarantine he did meet Calypso again - this time at a reception at the High Commissioner's Palace in San Anton. The reunion with Constance Spencer Smith must have caused him considerable embarrassment for the task of disentangling himself from love's snares was not an easy one and he had to resort to the 'most diabolical of explanations', as he put it in a letter to Lady Melbourne, his confidante. One wonders what these explanations were – though I wouldn't put it past Byron to have mentioned to the lady his many affairs and intrigues while he was gallivanting about in Greece and Albania. Constance for her part took her leave of the poet, kept his emerald ring and sailed 'up the Adriatic', while he boarded the frigate Volage bound for England, somewhat reluctant to return home to sort out his 'inadjustable affairs'.

Lord Byron

THE PASSION AND THE OOM PA PA

Andrew Alamango

The charming Valletta neighbourhood known as L-Arċipierku, or more specifically the corner strapped between the steps of St. Ursula street and Ta' Ġieżu church on St. John street, is a landmark for religious devotees, who every Easter flock to this part of town for a rather uncommon, heightened musical-religious experience – the Good Friday procession, the oldest one on the island dating back to 1646. In the afternoon, a large crowd amasses outside the church, spilling up and down the steps and streets, awaiting the start of the procession at 5pm.

Standing mid-way on the steps of St. Ursula one can gain an optimal overhead view of the unusual happenings down below; an ecclesiastical parade exits the highly revered church of Ta' Ġiezu, the beginning of a three and a half-hour procession trailing through the reverent streets of the city on an early spring evening, to be met with a 60-strong brass band which awaits at the bottom of the street's stairway, ready to provide the musical accompaniment for the evening.

The air tingles with anticipation as crowds continue to arrive and show their devotion, a fulfilment of their votive promises in the sacred shadows of the eight-statue procession; a guilt and sorrow-laden process, leading to the inevitable ecstasy and euphoria of resurrection two days later.

As is typical of southern Mediterranean Catholicism and its connected musical traditions, bi-polar extremities intertwine with drama and ceremony, in a play of dark and light, reminiscent of Caravaggio's carnal portrayals of divine happenings. The barefoot statue-bearers offer to carry the one-tonne, divinely inspired personifications, alongside the party of chain-dragging, crucifix-bearing, hooded sinners, in the hope of redemption through a process of total subjugation and pain.

The ceremony offers a social-theatre en plein air, with townsfolk in costume interpreting the most famous and infamous of biblical characters. They solemnly escort the fated statues laden with funeral wreaths and heavy damask, a costume tradition passed on through family lineage, accompanied by the stomp

17

and sway of the marching band.

Armed and ready with brass, woodwind and percussion instruments, the renowned La Vallette band plays out melancholic and sombre *mea culpa* dirges, referred to as *marċ funebri*.

The first Maltese band associations were formed in the 1860s and have their origins in military brass bands prevalent in the day. Stylistically redolent of Sicilian and southern Italian brass bands, they were initially non-religious, but by the early 1900s their primary function was that of accompanying the various religious activities in village celebrations and feasts. The brass band repertoire consists mainly of upbeat marches, polkas and waltzes. Band and parish rivalry has resulted in a lineage of local composers from the early 20th century who wrote flowery and lyrical funereal marches, which are played to this very day, alongside some of the better-known Sicilian pieces. Funeral bands accompanied most funerals, until the automobile brought about the demise of the horse-drawn hearse and outpaced the band-members. In more recent times funerary stomps became reserved solely for the accompaniment of state funerals, or band members.

The slow two-step marches are based on dramatic, operatic-style melodies and themes made popular through the dissemination of Italian culture since the nineteenth century. Generally in a two or four beat measure, the compositions are in lamenting minor keys, with opulent motifs and melodic and harmonic modulations simulating the rich damask tapestries that hang off the devotional statues (*il-vari*).

Trailing after the majestic statue of a flagellated Christ figure in his crown of thorns, the two-step pace is set by the melancholic un-snared drums, whilst dramatic operatic themes are churned out by teams of teasing clarinets, piccolo flutes, and soprano saxes, backed by the sombre stomp of the baritone tuba. The hypnotically woven, medium-range harmonies are subservient to a tragicomic, mariachi-style trumpet, broken only by the culminating splash of crash cymbals. Almost unexpectedly, the march breaks into an upbeat B section in a major key, contrasting, mocking almost, as in a Tim Burton twist of fate.

A sea of flat-topped white hats slow-march with a dangerously dizzying sway of delirium, as a wave of devotion and sacred incense sweep through the awe-struck crowds. In a Felliniesque display of riches, redemption and sorrow, the ecclesiastical troupe make their way through the dense streets and overbearing Baroque buildings, like a scene from Martin Scorsese's Godfather.

Marċi funebri die-hards scurry excitedly to the edges of the marching band, whistling the dramatic tunes, wishing they could be played on every day of the year. As procession and band make their way up St. Ursula Street they slowly disappear, turning left towards St Paul's street, stopping at the corners of the chess board streets as is custom for the Valletta procession. As the music and drama recedes in the fading light, I turn back up the steps, humming to myself, and return to the Valletta I know with an echo of solemn melancholy still in my heart.

Opposite page: Awaiting the Good Friday procession on St. John Street

David Pisani

STRADA STRETTA

Geoffrey Aquilina Ross
Illustration
Steph von Reiswitz

For many decades, when Britain's illustrious navy used the island as headquarters of its formidable Mediterranean Fleet, naval ratings coming ashore from ships in Marsamxett and the Grand Harbour gravitated immediately towards Valletta's infamous red light street where egg-and-chips were on the menus and friendly, young women offered their comforting presences. With wives and girlfriends safely at home in Blighty, the sailors were lured into this sleazy, narrow street in pursuit of the pleasures of the here-and-now with beer, food and women. Especially women. The money from their pay packets brought momentary wealth to the impoverished neighbourhood. In peacetime and war, these sailors were the mainstay of the street's economy.

By any standards the street was a slum. It always was. By the time World War 2 had faded into foggy memory, the lives of many residents had sunk to subsistence levels. Poverty and the deprivations of war had not been kind to either the buildings or the residents. Most had dreams of a better life elsewhere but until fortune smiled their way, they were constrained to live in tenements that were squalid, often in seedy individual rooms, with tap water rarely a constant commodity and with sanitation, such as it was, at the barest minimum. In was not unusual for one toilet in an open courtyard on the ground floor to serve the whole building.

By turning their street into a selection of bars with good-time girls to entertain every man, the residents had found a way to make money. Visitors, not condemned to living there, were seduced by the promises on offer. For the servicemen the street was The Gut, an abbreviation of The Gutter, a nickname bestowed by the British that was as appropriate as it was affectionate; low life meant fun.

Valletta's residents, naturally, clung to its given name that was in Italian, Strada Stretta (Strait Street). They took no pleasure in its reputation and regarded its presence as an unsavoury reality. For them, this alleyway bare of any architectural interest was best avoided, and even though it was just a few paces from the city's main street with fine clubs, shops and cafés catering for middle class families, they could comfortably ignore its existence. The street only sprung fully into life in the long hours of darkness anyway, when barmaids would lean on doorways touting for business, decorative lights would be switched on, and the tawdriness of the environment was masked by a sense of liberated jollity. If drunken sailors chose to be there by night, that was their business.

Members of the Army and the Royal Air Force stationed in barracks across the island made their way there too. As did sailors of other friendly nation's fleets when they called in at the island's harbours. And with nightlife almost non-existent elsewhere, many Maltese men made up the numbers. Here they could join the throng and dance and watch floor shows paying less, of course, than the foreign visitors.

With such a mixed clientele, drunken fights would often break out, spilling into the streets. Naval Shore Patrols and the Military Police were on duty every night to enforce the peace and arrest everyone who got out of hand.

In its narrow confines were a variety of smoky bars and dance halls where small bands played and exotic foreign women performed cabarets. Transvestite performers were popular too. Among the names that enticed visitors for dancing and a cabaret were the Egyptian Queen, Old Vic Cabaret, Lord Nelson Music Hall and, around the corner, the New Life Music Hall. At the Rexford the clientele was mostly Maltese. Among the favoured tiny bars were the Silver Horse, Smiling Prince, Tico-Tico, Blue Peter and Dirty Dicks. On the street on duty were boys and girls, as young as nine or ten, selling cigarettes, chewing gum and nuts. There was even a small lodging house called Cape of Good Hope. It was remarkable how much enterprise could be contained in such a small area. Available young women and dancing were the main attractions. Officially the women had to be 21 or older and each one had to be licenced by the police to work where alcohol was sold (Younger girls did work there too but, on being tipped off about an imminent police raid, hid in the background). A metal pin, a *midalja*, stamped with the initials MP (Malta Police) and a licence number had to be worm while working. Waiters and the foreign girls working in cabaret had similar badges. And each time a customer was coaxed by one of the women into buying drink, she earned herself a token, a *landa*. At closing time on a good night she might have earned four times a man's weekly wage.

Many of the working women and foreign performers were prostitutes, though not all. As early as 1898, the existence of prostitution, the engine that fired Strada Stretta, was acknowledged as a fact though brothels, as such, were banned. By 1920 a decree, the Venereal Disease Ordinance, was issued proclaiming that in future all prostitutes were to be medically examined four times a month by the government's Chief Medical Officer. Medical examinations were soon forgotten; brothels remain banned.

For some their entrance into the world's oldest profession began simply as a way to flirt with men and break away from the constraints of home life. But a considerable number were the daughters of prostitutes or daughters propelled into this vocation by their mothers in order to lift the family out of its poverty. Sometimes it was a son forced to take up this role.

In dwellings above the bars there were curtained cubicles where prostitutes could entertain their clients; their services charged on a sliding scale depending on the customer's nationality. In the final years of the street's slow decline of its red light business brought on by the Islands' declared Neutrality and the 1979 departure of the last of Britain's forces stationed in Malta, Maltese men paid £5, British sailors around £10, and US servicemen $20. Most women had a protector who took a portion of her earnings and ensured she was not mistreated by her clients. One such protector in recent memory was a woman.

With the sailors a distant memory and the garrison gone, the dance halls and bars ran out of business. Prostitution moved elsewhere and while many musicians who learned their skills the hard way went on to greater things, owning clubs or playing with their own bands at top hotels until disco music killed off dancing to live music, life for most of the denizens of The Gut who gave the street its lurid reputation was over.

Now, with street signs saying this is Triq id-Dejqa (Maltese for Strait Street), a revival is taking place driven by the realities of demand for inexpensive real estate at the centre of Valletta. Buildings are being restored. Wine bars, art galleries and restaurants are taking tentative steps towards its colonisation alongside offices and the Law Court annex that have already claimed their shares. The sleaziness that once there was has become a distant memory.

SCOT ON
SCOTS STREET

Andrew Gow

I have been to Malta twice – the first time I came passively; a sort of third-hand experience of the best possible kind. I remember protruding balconies, spires and a turquoise ferry with a German name that chugged across Marsamxett Harbour. But the stay was all planned out, event-filled, with not a single moment of solitude. The next time, I resolve, I will come here alone. I have been struck suddenly by the potential of being here by myself, believing that there could be nothing more exquisite than loneliness in Malta.

So the first visit demands its sequel and back in London I am emailing a man who owns an apartment block to negotiate the terms of a ten-day stay in May, or on a trip to the bank to make an international transfer, or booking a seat on an Air Malta plane (which bears a red Maltese cross on its tail). And it is with a sense of purpose that I return, if not to continue with some long overdue writing, then to become the author of this experience, to see Malta first hand.

But I should make clear that it is a very particular Malta that I have come back for. And it is by no means the only Malta that exists. Valletta is a place that could not be more exemplary of the kind of 'faded grandeur' you would expect to read about in Condé Nast Traveller. And yet it's the city's steep and ragged backstreets, its dirty, little corners that make me feel so peaceful. This is a place of dogs who walk contentedly down cobbled streets without their masters, of bold cats who choose to sleep in the sunspot in the centre of the street, of coffin-makers who feed the cats with chicken bones, and of silent virgins who watch benignly from encrusted alcoves. But, as I am reminded on my second outbound flight, Valletta is a place that doesn't charm everyone. It is low on shops and nightlife and has been abandoned by the island's younger dwellers in favour of Sliema and Saint Julian's, which offer bars, clubs and condominiums. As far as many young islanders are concerned, and perhaps rightly so, Valletta, the capital city and historic centre is backward, potentially emblematic of what might be wrong with Malta. But there it is: this is where I am undoubtedly most content. And yes, it's stressful having to justify this to the Hungarian woman sitting next to me on the plane. We're at thirty thousand feet and she's lecturing me on how I should be having more fun. It feels familiar. Oddly, this isn't the first time I've been forced to listen to someone ten years older than me, while in transit, who has the same recreational urges as my distant teenage self. She thinks I'd be far happier down the road in Saint Julian's. Oh yes, I remember wearily, somebody mentioned it to me once 'that stretch of coastline famed for its bars and clubs'. I laugh politely, feeling almost priggish, and explain that I'm not looking for that sort of holiday. But then there's an offer of snorkelling. As it turns out, she works at a jetty, or a surf shack - a place where I imagine her flanked by a group of hot neoprene-clad antipodeans. She's very enthusiastic, just got in from New York, she says. I was there last October, I reflect, and realised I didn't love it like I once thought I did. Maybe I don't love London anymore either. Maybe it's been a while since I loved London. But then I check myself because this sort of information can make for painful exchanges, especially with those still rapt by the manky grandeur of cities; the seductive horrors of the metropolis. It's what's known as 'oversharing', a sin I can be guilty of when searching for connections. But what she's suggesting to me wouldn't be a writerly sojourn, it would be an activities holiday. And the thought of activity at this point makes me die inside. But where did I go so wrong that I can no longer delight in such things, I am forced to ponder on my bus ride to Valletta from the airport.

The buses are wonderful by the way; all low-slung fifties shapes, artfully battered, bright yellow with an orange stripe. The circular bus terminal outside Valletta's City Gate, with its hubbub and palms, puts you in mind of any film about an American or Englishman abroad. If you walk to the top of the City Gate you can luxuriate shamelessly in this mise-en-scène. The buses on their roundabout pilgrimage, the Phoenicia hotel palpitating behind sprinklers, the palms, the flowers… The only thing missing is Jimmy Stewart in white linen, elegantly harassed by the agitation of a lively, exotic thoroughfare.

Well it's no wonder they choose to make so many films here. Looking at the recent ones, however, I can't help thinking most choose to ignore the precious and potent particularities of old Malta's civic charms. The studios come here for its ancient aridness, its megalithic virtues, the film studio tanks. And its rocks. Malta is an island all about rocks, they say. They also say it's important to understand this if you want to even begin understanding Malta. This is a sentiment held in affection by many members of the island's creative circles, who you might encounter in Valletta. Rocks are very esoteric of course; for many, they are not at all easy to relate to. Walls are the most primitive and elemental feature of Malta, and perhaps also its most rarefied. There is a book, *Walls of Malta*, published in 1973, by architect Richard England; in the foreword art historian A. C. Sewter writes that, 'in Malta the landscape itself is architectural, and the buildings are landscape'.

But your most intimate encounter with rocks is likely to be at the beach and it's highly probable you will be taken to a rock beach at some point. Like the Bay of St. Thomas where I was taken by two girls, E and V. There you will be forced to accept that there is no sand. You will strip off and lie reluctantly on hot hard rocks until your body yields to them like a slothful lizard, deciding to change colour to whatever it's sitting on.

I arrive in Valletta, my room is not quite what I expected – it faces into a dark street. The kitchen is basic: a dead roach in a salad bowl (though be warned, they're everywhere - as I later discover. There just aren't the resources to mount a mass-scale pest eradication in these old buildings), and there are fusty-smelling under-sink cupboards. Through the partitioning wall comes the sound of woodwind. An Italian oboist knocks on my door and introduces himself. He keeps his curtains drawn and has large eyebags that are perhaps testament to this. He apologises in advance for his daily arpeggios. But how can I be irritated? Having a reclusive musician next door is quaint. All very *Room With A View* without the view.

And where would I be without him after all? On my encounter with a large cockroach who I unsuccessfully try to trap between a glass and a nearby Times of Malta, but who manages to pincer up my forearms like a demon risolle, I unleash a catamite's scream loud enough to summon my neighbour, armed with a can of aerosol poison. He doesn't laugh at me for shrieking even though I feel I have to justify it. He's seen and done this before, he consoles me. We bond. And on discovery that there's Wi-Fi, well, I can't help but feel that my whole trip will be completely wasted. The point being to purge myself of internet distraction; to rid myself of the city just as urbanites do in books and movies. If I have access, I won't get anything done and will return to London feeling wretched and creatively impotent. I resort to asking the oboist to remove my browsers, as I can't quite bear to do it myself. Harsh but necessary.

The man who runs this building is theatrical and shares my taste in crockery. On my last day he offers me money for a salad bowl in the shape of a lettuce leaf which I picked up at the famous Birgu fleamarket, a Sunday event in Malta's weekly social diary attended by many of the island's expat creatives (either combing for movie props, or decorating their boho apartments). It'll remind you of the fleamarkets of Berlin, except you'll more likely return with Catholic bagatelle than Ostblock tchotchke. My landlord picks up an ashtray I bought. When I tell him where it's from, he is genuinely shocked: 'That place? P'uh!', holding it up in the afternoon sunlight with his strong fingers. He says he remembers these from childhood. He has a brother who's the handyman and the more macho version of him. It's interesting listening to them talk together. There's something mannered about their exchanges, nostalgic, essential, in such a way that I'd like to bottle and take back home with me. That language, Maltese, graphic Arabic edges rounded with romance gracenotes: Baħrija I say to myself in E's car as we drive to the fishing village of Marsaxlokk a couple of days later, Baħ-rrija, Baħrija, Mġarr, Mġarr. Learn to pronounce these, they're addictive. But it's the daytime walks around the city that I've come for too. When the others are at work, doing what they're doing, I saunter around, back to where I've been before and where I haven't ventured. The Lower Barakka gardens, where you can sit in the shade of a giant arch, or the Upper Barrakka gardens, where you can dodge wedding parties and look out across the Grand Harbour to Senglea, Vittoriosa and the dry docks, and below to the Valletta bastions flanked by the desolate grandeur of neighbouring Floriana, where E lives. Agreeably sized, Valletta is plotted on a grid-network of streets. Built over a steep promontory, the visitor must quickly devise strategies at minimising physical endurance. You will notice stucco crests and putti and burnished shopfronts with names like Spiteri and Azzopardi. The texture of some of these little emporia is exquisite, right down to the colour of cladding or tile. The place seems to be all about patina.

I go into a café appearing to be favoured by locals. They serve pastries, pies and the local *pastizzi*, the clam or lozenge shaped flaky pastry. It's impossible to know what's in any of them and I'm embarrassed at the prospect of ordering one that might be full of dense meat-ness, or worse still, egg, which I don't fancy consuming in full view of everyone. Asking in my heightened state of self-consciousness doesn't feel like an option, so I go for a more demure-looking confection. It's spinach and ricotta, but the texture is decidedly more parched than you might expect. This is not an epicurean's island, not in the way you might expect from somewhere so close to Italy.

Needless to say the Maltese identity is markedly separate from their neighbouring nations. Admirable too perhaps is that there's little ambition here to be like Italy. If truth be known the Maltese are probably more like the British, having asked for British rule following Napoleon's defeat. And everywhere you will see vestiges of this epoch: red pillar boxes, 19th century tenements that look like they could be lifted out of Glasgow's west end.

But later I see something that genuinely shocks me. Words. 'Vagina', 'virgin mary', 'valium', 'vain', 'vague', all plastered in whorish red across a vitrine on the corner of Strait Street and Old Theatre street. What is this, a strip-club, I wonder? Oh wait a second, it's ironic. But right next to the town square? It's an arts space masquerading as a louche, red enclave with a black man standing at the door in a dickie bow. On closer inspection it's a public convenience, and the man is really a toilet attendant, forced to swelter here in his woollen suit. Inside is the familiar scrawl of *Tracey Emin*, a neon declaration of love to said artist, by another artist. Baffling. So what, you are left thinking, is one to make of this? Just where do you begin to unpack the mangled meanings of this curiosity, with its glibly provocative signage and unfortunate reminders of this country's residual racism?

Valletta is discovering po-mo, the easy allure of reconstruction, marrying scarred biblical walls with stainless steel fittings. But of course, you can't be too precious about such things. There is no reason this place should be hermetically preserved. The niggling feeling remains, however, that somebody could definitely be doing the job better, perhaps with more class.

Perhaps because I am in search of loneliness it is difficult to find it. I have never felt more social than in Malta. 'Social' in a way that I think my grandmother from the Eastern block thinks of the word. Civilised, regular. Seeing friends in cafés, sitting in the square after lunch. I can't do that back home. I always meet up with V whom I know already from London, and E, who is Maltese. We'll drive down winding roads at night, the three of us, and talk, really talk, until we pull up at the side of the road to take us on a conversation journey that the car just can't keep up with. We give in to our heads and the synergy between us.

Almost every night we will claim a little seating enclave at the Maestro Bar on South Street and look out onto the street. I'll drink beers, smoke other people's rollies and feel giddily drunk, self-indulgently cosmopolitan. On my first evening there a sensitive, bearded American tells me that these backwaters have become the new spiritual home for the itinerant artistic soul. That night I'll dream about Iowa and random snowy townships in Canada. Silly really, because the whole point of coming here was for exactly the sense of remoteness we have spent most of the night discussing.

On my last night, there's a party to celebrate V's birthday, at a tiki bar in St. Paul's Bay. E drives us back, down black roads, with electric flies leaping from the fields into the electric glare of the headlights. The morning beckons and I look out from V's bedroom window as she sleeps, onto a stormy, summer sea. Clouds merge with a cobalt torsion of spray and rock. And yes, for a while, perhaps it is loneliness that I feel while I look out at this. The loneliness that I thought I wanted, but strangely don't yearn for anymore.

UNSEEN SLIEMA: A GUIDE TO THE INVISIBLE ATTRACTIONS

Raphael Vassallo

They say it can still be seen on certain days of the year: a faint glow of electric blue reflected in the dusty asphalt of Tower Road, and sometimes on the orange flanks of buses as they turn up the hill from the Ferries.

It is visible to all, so long as you know where to look. The secret is in the trees. What unnatural force, what tortured hiccup of the earth, could have caused them to recoil in such horror from the square's outer lip, as if shielding their countless pigeons from the nameless monstrosity below? Look more closely. Clear your mind of questions. Block out the surrounding buildings, the sound of traffic, everything but the trees – no, block out the trees too – and slowly the presence will start to take shape.

And what shape! Small wonder the taxi drivers would mind their heads and the bus drivers shield their eyes. For as its name so aptly implies, the Magic Kiosk that once stood on St Anne's Square was both difficult and dangerous to ignore. And the magic was nothing if not unpredictable. One day it might suddenly extend a limb to claim an open-air veranda, which it would later cover in glass to protect cappuccinos from falling leaves and pigeon guano. The next time you looked, a whole new gun-turret would have sprouted from the roof, shooting bright red Coca-Cola adverts at regular intervals across the broad expanse of the Ferries.

And on the kiosk grew, in a series of random, clunky expansions, slowly blocking from view the entire square: trees, neighbouring kiosk, Majestic Cinema and all until, in true tragic hero fashion, it finally overreached itself, and the bulldozers came and tore it down in 2009.

Tim Machin

St Anne's Square

There are many good reasons why the resulting St Anne's Square would mark the natural starting point for any self-respecting tour of Sliema's unseen attractions: not least because it didn't quite exist as a square until only very recently.

In a sense, you could say this is true of Sliema as a whole – a town which also didn't quite exist until it 'hastily from the coast arose' in the late 19th century - and perhaps it also mirrors the history of Malta, being a tale that makes sense only when viewed through the inscrutable prism of local politics.

Like all Sliema's myriad apartment blocks, the Magic Kiosk had arisen from the dust of a hastily demolished antecedent – a much smaller and less obtrusive kiosk that had been run by the same family for years. And like so many other stories involving property across the island, its transfer was acrimonious. Officially, the new proprietor had won the public tender fair and square, the previous lease having duly expired in 1973. Unofficially, the lease had been terminated for purely political reasons, and the new one engineered under purely 'exceptional' circumstances (one newspaper reports that the gift exchange ritual involved a silver teapot to which the Lands Minister of the time retorted: "A teapot? Not what I expected. Get me Lm25,000! [around €60,000] You have one week!")

To be fair, no national consensus has ever evolved on the integrity or otherwise of this transaction. But either way, the Magic Kiosk was quickly transformed by popular imagination into the least likely thing imaginable: a visible manifestation of Malta's eternally irresolvable political divide, at a time when the division itself was at its most volatile. How else to explain the fact that its demolition came to occupy a prime time slot on Television Malta's 8 o'clock news? And that the subsequent 'liberation' of St Anne's Square came accompanied by both media scrum and unofficial street party? Not for nothing did the admirers of seventies kitsch – especially the mainly British expat community, which associated the place with breakfast rather more than with politics - lament the essentially political nature of its demise. "Only in Malta could the future of a cafe be brought down to the level of gutter politics," was one complaint on an online chat forum, as the bulldozers rolled in.

And yet it is a story that repeats itself, albeit with variations, in practically every nook and cranny of Sliema. Similar transactions (often involving similar gift exchange rituals) have since opened the floodgates to a seemingly never-ending construction boom. Any given street could sprout any number of treacherous obstructions, usually involving massive concrete blocks to support steel tower cranes – some of which have occasionally been known to topple during fierce north-easterly gales, or sudden craters where there had once been a row of identical townhouses.

On any given day as many as 16 such cranes can be observed leering above Sliema's uneven skyline. And from our vantage point on St Anne's Square, the results of their endeavours can be appreciated in the form of a long, shiny strip of shopping centres, showrooms, hotels and apartment blocks rising above the waterfront like a line of broken teeth.

But here we are concerned with Sliema's less conspicuous features, and for this reason St Anne's Square provides an admirable point of departure. For what better location to observe the township's most glaring unseen presence, than reflected on the placid waters of Marsamxett?

The Ferries

Despite an entirely understandable misconception, 'going to the ferries' is not a local euphemism for shuffling off one's mortal coil. On the contrary it is very much an affirmation of life; for if there ever was a single pulsing heart within the town of Sliema, it would have to be the wide expanse of reclaimed land on the northern littoral of Marsamxett harbour, facing Manoel Island and the Valletta bastions beyond.

St Anne's Square irrupts onto the precise epicentre of this esplanade, and from under its ficus trees the reasons for its centrality to Sliema life become plain to see. Being south-facing, the Ferries is a place blessed by sunlight, its borders defined by a bustling shopping centre on one side, and a broad seafront promenade on the other. It is the reason for Sliema's continued allure and the ever burgeoning parking problems.

Ironically the Magic Kiosk itself contributed to both these phenomena. Born of the island's political divide, it was a creature formally boycotted by the vast majority of Sliema residents throughout the 1980s – when buying a Kinnie from that place, even at the bargain price of 2c 3mils, was deemed an act of treachery against *religio et patria*. Such was its magic, though, that it succeeded in summoning from afar a new patronage of an altogether different political hue, surviving the boycott comfortably and cementing the area's status as 'the place to be' for succeeding generations (for a time, the Ferries became an unwise place to loudly air one's political convictions).

Even to this day such open proclamations are sometimes best avoided; for though the simmering political tensions of yesteryear have subsided, other tensions still occasionally erupt... and it is to the Ferries that throngs of festooned football supporters from all over the island will invariably descend, celebrating with noisy abandon their own team's latest triumph, or likelier still, the humiliation of their most detested rivals.

Depending on the circumstances, therefore, 'going to the ferries' can just as easily imply a shopping spree at Zara's, British Homestores or Anastasi Brothers Domestic Appliances; an afternoon lounge over a coffee at La Rive (if you're hip) or Tony's Bar (if you're interested in the local gossip); or getting swept away by a typically Maltese festivity of mass jubilation and dangerous driving if you can put up with the noise.

Admittedly, though, it can no longer mean a visit to the 'Talkies', as it did for so long – all three of Sliema's landmark cinemas having long since bitten the construction dust – and it certainly will not refer to any of the ferryboats which once gave the place its name, bridging the gap between Sliema and the so-called 'other side' (both of the harbour, and of an unspoken political frontier). These have all long since been spirited away, and with them went the complex system of boarding jetties and gangways to make space for the seafront promenade. Today, only two modes of maritime transportation are still available across Marsamxett port: the bright red fleet of pirate vessels belonging to Captain Morgan (who has since retired from looting and pillaging, and now offers harbour cruises instead); and a single ferryboat servicing the Valletta route.

The Front

For obvious reasons, The Ferries once marked the first point of entry for almost all visitors to Sliema's shores, and as such it is to be expected that several options would be open to the newly alighted. Those wishing to leave Sliema at once would be well advised to follow the Strand along the waterfront towards Gżira, though the precise point at which Sliema is left behind, and Gżira entered, is one that not even the very wise have been able to ascertain. For the rest, the traditional approach would be to walk up the incline of Tower Road to the junction with Bisazza Street, then turn left before enjoying a leisurely

Balluta Buildings

stroll along the 'Peace Promenade', to use the official name by which the Front is never known.

If the Ferries is Sliema's beating heart, The Front can certainly claim to be its main peripheral axon. A long, tamarisk-lined promenade, punctuated by benches and dotted with many a magic kiosk, it will take you past the length of Sliema all the way to the neighbourhoods of Balluta and St Julian's. Again, the precise transition point between all three is largely a matter of guesswork. Some maintain that Balluta is entered at a point midway between the Taormina Kiosk and the Barracuda Restaurant, both overlooking the broad expanse of St Julian's Bay. Others argue that one must continue past the Barracuda restaurant until in sight of the inlet's most striking landmarks: the single lone Norfolk Island pine-tree standing sentinel above the shore (an unassuming guard at the Le Méridien Hotel?) and the grand presence of Balluta Buildings, an art nouveau extravaganza, on the opposite corner of the bay.

In any case, by now will you have left Sliema firmly behind, even if your one-mile trek never once strayed from Tower Road (though it is about to, as the same road suddenly becomes Grenfell Street at an indeterminate point somewhere past *The City Of London* bar). And for much the same reason, a stroll along the Front is also probably the best way to visit Sliema without actually seeing the place at all. For though nearly all the promenade falls squarely within that town's confines, its Sliema-facing border is fronted by the same line of broken-teeth buildings that have so successfully shielded the town from view everywhere else. Besides, it is also a traditional venue of choice for the summer evening family *passiġġjata*: which means that for roughly five months of the year, the Peace Promenade will be invaded at dusk by all manner of infiltrators - strollers, joggers, cyclists, tricyclists, skateboarders, rollerbladers, dog-walkers and pushchairs.

Nonetheless it is a picturesque walkway, as can be attested by the fact that is has starred in so many moving pictures. Apart from putting in an appearance alongside Roger Moore in an episode of The Saint (1969), and Paul Newman in The Mackintosh Man (1973), Sliema's Peace Promenade more recently doubled up as a section of the Tel Aviv waterfront, complete with plans for a covert Mossad anti-terrorist operation, in Steven Spielberg's Munich (2005).

It is naturally debatable whether Spielberg was aware at the time that all this was old hat to a seafront promenade that has witnessed much over the past century or so. A decade before Geoffrey Rush and Eric Bana took that stroll past Surfside Bar and Restaurant, and just across the road outside the Diplomat Hotel, unidentified assailants on motorbikes had already gunned down Faati Al-Shqaqi, founder of Jihad Islamica, in October 1995.

At most other times, however, the Peace Promenade is every bit as peaceful as the name suggests... except perhaps when territorial disputes break out between the many different factions vying for right of way. At the time of writing, hostility has just been declared between cyclists and strollers, and a verdict from the local council is expected 'shortly'. Last year, it was joggers and rollerbladers; the year before, footballs and dog poop. Visitors are further advised that this is also the route favoured by the traditional festive carcade - be it in celebration of politics, football or waterpolo - and not without good reason either: the Sliema Front neatly skirts the entire town, thereby maximising the radius in which residents will have no option but to put up with the honking of horns.

All things told, there is never really a dull moment on the Peace Promenade. But whether it can be counted among Sliema's attractions, or dismissed as an alien hinterland around its outermost borders, is another question entirely.

Cathedral Street

To experience the town that lies hidden behind this thick outer crust, we must retrace our steps to St Anne's Square, and this time turn left far before that corner with Bisazza Street, up Cathedral Street instead.

Fortunately it is difficult to get lost, for Cathedral Street distinguishes itself from any other similarly named street by means of one unique detail: the tell-tale lack of any visible cathedral. To be fair, the Stella Maris parish church does try to atone for this by jutting a single belfry up from the precise summit of the hill; and so successful is its effort that ill-informed visitors have been known to assume that Stella Maris is indeed the reason for the street's name, despite having its own eponymous street on the downward slope of the hill, slicing through Sliema like a knife on its way to the Gelateria Lungomare, and the seafront beyond. However, any resident of the area will happily inform them it is actually named after Cathedral Library: the long defunct stationery that once sat across the road from St Joseph's secondary school for girls, and introduced Hallmark and Mills & Boon to the collective conscious of an entire generation. Yet the truth is that the entire plot on which this town so hastily arose was once the property of St John's co-Cathedral in Valletta.

Whatever the reason, the street itself marks a clear transition from the waterfront hinterland and the town it surrounds; and the higher you climb up the hill, the clearer this transition becomes. Traffic (except early afternoons on schooldays) is altogether less congested here than at the Ferries, and shops are much fewer. Gone too is the 'high street' feel of the shops themselves, though ironically High Street is in fact our current destination: the backbone of central Sliema, and once the town's main thoroughfare until usurped by the coastal upstarts. Now you will pass less contemporary outlets such as the locksmith who has cut all this part of Sliema's spare front-door keys for decades. The unkempt of hair may pause to admire Combs Unisex Salon, which both shears its patrons and regales them with classic rock numbers from the 1970s, the album covers adorning the walls like trophies. Towards the top of the hill is the semi-underground lotto booth, with its never-ending queues on Super Five Wednesdays; and on Sunday mornings, the narrow Stella Maris parvis directly overhead will be alive with people popping in and out of church, or to and from the Golden Harvest across the road for their fresh bread, newspapers and cigarettes.

Of the houses in between, some even have front porches - a rarity throughout the island, in spring they are cluttered with geraniums and, appropriately enough, with the plant we refer to as Stella Maris. Though Cathedral street itself is currently a hive of ongoing construction activity, its tributary streets are narrow and quiet, for the most part overlooked by twin regiments of brightly coloured wooden balconies. It is not inconceivable to see the occasional wicker basket being lowered or raised from one of these balconies, as was standard up until a few decades ago; and the local fishmonger still loudly proclaims his wares at the back of an open lorry at the top of the hill (though he has reluctantly had to invest in an onboard fridge-freezer, in conformity with EU directives).

But while snatches of an all but extinct lifestyle can clearly still be discerned in and about Cathedral street, Sliema as a whole is perhaps not the best place to look for nostalgic reminiscences of a forgotten Malta. The pace of its recent changes has been dictated not just by a powerful construction lobby, but also by demographics: the town itself being apparently locked in a permanent cycle of de- and re-population. By turns fashionable and unfashionable a residential enclave, Sliema admits and releases its newcomers and emigrants in regular waves; and what was true of previous generations – that Sliema is by definition a seaside resort, or a Nationalist stronghold, or that its inhabitants tend to speak English more than others – is not always true of subsequent ones; or at least, not in total, and never for very long.

The Three Trees, pivotal road axis.

It is said that once it was possible to step into the front garden of a house on what is now High street, and out of its backdoor onto what is now Bisazza street, though four blocks have since arisen in between. Some of these original houses still survive, and even those that have long disappeared can sometimes still be discerned: such as when a small corner of what was once a private garden outlives its original form to become a seminal landmark – like the Three Trees.

Visitors to this spot, walking left on High street, will

'The Three Trees'

quickly note that only one of the original three trees still stands today. Of the fate of the other two trees, none can now say with any certainty. But locals still talk of the Three Trees to signify that pivotal roundabout upon which Sliema's busiest inner roads now converge: Rudolf and High streets, which combine to form a West-East axis along the highest point of Sliema's ridge; and Dingli and St Mary's streets, which slope off downwards in opposite directions. A word of warning: we are now at the core of Sliema's central nervous system, where nerves are often exacerbated by the impossible task of wrapping all incoming traffic around one island roughly the size of a dinner table.

It is on this roundabout that the sole survivor of the Three Trees still stands, flourishing, despite exhaust fumes, in a magnificent profusion of green above a single, bright red telephone box. Viewed from High Street, the One Tree seems to rise directly out of the phone box itself: an optical illusion, of course, but inquisitive passersby wishing to make sure – or for that matter to make a telephone call - are advised to approach the tree with caution. Not only is the crossing perilous, but the telephone box itself, complete with its GIIR insignia, has a tendency to be hurtled across the road and into the grocery on the corner, as one motorist after another miscalculates the impossible manoeuvre around its island. Yet no one has ever thought to move it from its current location; after each succeeding accident it is promptly replaced and repainted, not so much in deference to King George, but because it is the only inland public phone-box this part of Sliema has to offer: the nearest alternative being all of five minutes away on foot. In any case, on this particular visit we shall admire the Three Trees only from a safe distance, before turning right off High Street down the north-facing slope of Sliema ridge.

Ġorġ Borg Olivier House

Victoria Avenue

An up-to-date map is essential to navigate the back streets of Sliema. The reason has less to do with the size or even complexity of the town's otherwise labyrinthine streetscape – you can easily walk the length and breadth of Sliema in twenty minutes – than with the curious tendency of the streets themselves to unexpectedly change name.

In most cases, entire sections of the town would have been arbitrarily selected for rechristening by Malta's official 'national street-naming committee', comprising a panel of experts in various topics such as: obscure Maltese flora and fauna; farming and navigational implements; saints, bishops, popes and priests; and the occasional personality of yore (mostly politicians and former chief justices). Fortunately Sliema was spared any experts of the 'vegetable, mineral, animal and thing' variety, so none of its residents suddenly found themselves domiciled on 'Artichoke', 'Limestone', 'Wheelbarrow' or 'Lesser Small-Eared Bat' street, as has been known to be happen in other localities. But personalities of yore are another matter, and people who had lived all their lives on New or Parallel streets are still perplexed by the fact that they one day awoke on Sir Arturo Mercieca and Sir Luigi Pelligrini street instead.

For instance: tourists are often amused when told that they have to "go up the Prince of Wales" to get to the Sliema police station. But their amusement turns to frustration when they slowly realise that there is no longer any road by this name. Yet its official name, Manwel Dimech street, is to this day resisted. Here, too, the magic of the kiosk is at work behind the scenes: for while the Prince of Wales was a suitably neutral and non-aligned entity in divided Malta, the choice of Manwel Dimech as usurper was made by the same Labour government that was so ardently boycotted in the 1980s. Historians will quickly point out that this is unfair on Manwel Dimech, a maverick political activist, exiled to Egypt long before the Labour Party was founded. But truth be told, the local resistance to change is about more than just politics. For even streets renamed after politicians from the 'preferred' political formation – in this case, the Nationalist Party – are also still called by their earlier, British names, even when the snubbed politicians in question happened to have lived on those streets for years.

Ġorġ Borg Olivier street is a perfect example. By all accounts it is a more cogent name than the one it replaced – Victoria Avenue – for unlike the British Empress, Borg Olivier himself was once prime minister of Malta, and his house still stands halfway up the hill, adjacent to the Capua Palace Hospital. But in the battle for street name supremacy, Victoria has always emerged victorious; for not only is the name Borg Olivier Street rarely heard in Sliema, but its more recent additions have cemented the monarch's long reign by calling themselves things like The Victoria Hotel.

The latter is today Victoria Avenue's most conspicuous feature, and standing on its threshold near the corner with High Street – a stone's throw from the Three Trees – one can for a moment appreciate the results of some three generations of Sliema's staggered attempts at 'high-rise' construction: from the Tower Palace Hotel at the foot of the hill, built during Malta's very earliest mass-tourism drive in the 1960s; to the altogether more recent apartments blocks huddled around the corner with Capua street; to the Capua Hospital, rising from the estate of the eponymous 19th century palace which happily survived (if only just) a direct demolition attempt in the early 1990s. And peering down the length of Victoria Avenue from High Street are two of the town's better preserved *villeġġjatura* homes: Fatima House (formerly Villa Betheram), and Villino Zammit, both of which retain their densely-fronded front gardens, and are practically invisible from any angle save directly in front, hemmed in at all corners by tight clusters of concrete tower blocks.

Viewers are naturally free to make their own artistic appraisals of the results. One thing they will certainly remark, however, is the unique character of the Borg Olivier residence itself: recognisable at a glance by a large marble plaque by the front door; and also by the battlements on its roof, the narrow-slit windows from which to fire projectiles, and a host of other warlike features clearly designed to withstand a siege.

This is by no means accidental, for it is not unheard of (at least in decades gone by) for private homes of politicians to be redecorated with a bright splash of red or blue paint – or even to be besieged at intervals by cohorts from the enemy camp. Anecdotes of such attacks, often as not featuring grandmothers evacuated to safety over neighbouring rooftops, are still routinely trotted out as cautionary tales before every election; and though it is now but a distant memory, the grotesque parade by Labour enthusiasts up Victoria Avenue in 1971, when Borg Olivier was defeated by the Labour Party's Dom Mintoff, has never been fully forgotten or forgiven. But, if any direct attack was made on the edifice itself, it left no visible mark on its outer defences. Those battlements have clearly served their purpose well, and now that Borg Olivier dwells there no longer, it is unlikely they shall be called into action any time soon.

To Reno Bar, and beyond

Short of inventing a time machine, the quickest way to catch a glimpse of Sliema in the 1970s and 1980s is to pop onto Howard Street around the corner for a quiet drink at Reno Bar.

'Quiet' in this instance is a relative term. Reno's is admittedly not over fond of loud music, though there are occasional exceptions: usually involving a rare victory for Sliema Wanderers, in a football league now largely dominated by Valletta and Birkirkara. But discussions around the bar can be vocal and animated affairs, especially when dealing with any of the area's traditionally 'burning' topics: football, parking, exploits of the local council, an apparent spike in recent street crime, and of course the recent activities of Sliema's stealthiest and most dangerous predator, the traffic warden. All such topics are to be raised here with caution, for the purveyors of Reno's Bar are undisputed experts in all that touches thereupon. Now drawing towards its 50th anniversary, Reno's is, in a sense, the repository of the ancestral wisdom of three succeeding generations of *Sliemiżi*, and from their collective memories – which they are usually happy to share with all who gravitate there – much can be learnt about the town's many intrigues.

But Reno's Bar (and now also confectionary) evokes the past in other ways, too. No matter how brightly the sun beats down on the road outside, the moment you step under its olive green canopy you will find yourself instantly

SLIEMA +
ST. JULIANS

ST. ANNE'S SQUARE

THE FERRIES

STELLA MARIS

DIPLOMAT HOTEL

RENO'S BAR

THREE TREES

BALLUTTA BUILDINGS

teleported into a nether world of permanent dusk. Indeed, this uncanny ability to repel even the brightest sunshine has been the marvel of many a passing astrophysicist; and the phenomenon seems to work with artificial light too; the place seems to swim in a murky haze of darkness, broken only by the occasional flicker of light reflected in the myriad bottles above the bar.

Once your eyes grow accustomed to the dark, their next task will be to assimilate the sheer preponderance of oddities that Reno's Bar has accumulated over the long years. For though it has changed little since 1961, Reno's - much like Sliema as a whole - is not exactly a place where time stands still. At one point it lost its games room at the back, dashing the pool-playing or darts-throwing ambitions of many a youngster. Instead it gained a dazzling array of freezers packed with ice creams, as well as an ever-burgeoning wine-rack, and shelves upon shelves of glistening packets of Twistees and other savoury snacks. But all these new additions are always somehow accommodated around the surplus of what was already there, so that despite its permanent dusk the place somehow always feels full and alive, even when relatively devoid of people.

Stepping out after your quiet drink, it is not uncommon to be momentarily blinded by the forgotten sunlight, and this, too, will be vaguely familiar to any who have lived in Sliema back in the days when the Magic Kiosk expanded on St Anne's Square; the entire town was often as not plunged into darkness for hours on end, as Malta's only (and long obsolete) power station in Marsa groaned under the strain of furnishing the islands with power. There are conflicting explanations for this state of affairs. Officially, electricity (and also running water, the two being inextricably linked) had to be judicially rationed owing to the difficulties of its production. Sliema residents, however, will point out that their locality was sacrificed far more frequently than others – and a cursory glance and blackout statistics for those times will powerfully argue their case.

Either way, the typical Sliema household will to this day always keep at least one paraffin lamp in reserve, as well as a drawer-full of candles, torches and matches, and perhaps this is just as well, for two decades and one new power station later, electricity is still an occasionally unreliable ally, though its regular suspension is perhaps less selective than in previous years.

Dingli Circus

As it is in the nature of one memory to evoke another, and as Howard Street leads inexorably from Reno's Bar to Dingli Street, it is perhaps fitting to end this tour at the place where all such injustices, real or perceived, are traditionally protested against by thousands. For if the Ferries or the Front are points of mass convergence in times of celebration, in other times of rebellion or popular angst, the place to air one's frustration is invariably Dingli Circus, between the Three Trees at the top of the hill, and Balluta bay at the bottom.

As circuses go, this one has disappointed many a child with its lack of visible clowns, elephants, tigers and trapeze artists. But at moments the name has nonetheless been curiously apt. There is, after all, something essentially burlesque about Malta's culture of political 'mass meetings' – those heaving swarms of red or blue coloured multitudes, gathered under flags and placards to roar their allegiance to one party or the other – and this quality seems to magnify in direct proportion to the level of discontent. Themes may be improvised, depending on the grievance of the moment: so that when protesting the water shortage in the 1980s, supporters attended wielding empty buckets and toilets made of papier-mâché; and during the church school crisis of 1984, uniformed school children were paraded through the streets under slogans such as 'SOS: Save Our Schools'. No matter the chosen theme, children and toddlers will be wrapped up in party handkerchiefs and held aloft, bewildered, above the heaving crowds. All will have come to hear their master's voice; and the message shall always be noisily appreciated, no matter how little it actually changes over the years.

Looking at Dingli Circus today, it is difficult to envisage a largely traffic-free time when as many as 80,000 (claimed) or 30,000 (more likely) people would file in from all corners of the island – transported by coaches, sometimes wheeled out of retirement homes or borne from hospitals on stretchers – to make up the numbers for a show of force. And yet, when viewed from the roof of the Metropole Hotel, there were times when Dingli street appeared like an animated river of deepest blue: its tributaries streaming in from all directions, and its waving flags forming currents and eddies on the surface as the bellowing of party leaders echoed about its shores. And while mass meeting fervour has diminished somewhat in the meantime (the chances of dispersal by tear gas, or being hit by a stray rubber bullet, being considerably more remote these days) that same blue river still wells up every five or so years in Dingli street – and just as regularly, rivers of red flow through the main thoroughfares of other towns.

And once the tide ebbs and the multitudes return to their homes and hospitals, Dingli street and environs will emerge from the shadows to pick up the pieces they left behind - the beer bottles, foghorns and heaps of strewn confetti – and invariably Sliema will revert to its own unique pace of change. Sometimes it changes hastily, sometimes leisurely; constantly being reinvented into something different, though never entirely new.

A Nationalist Party mass meeting.

43

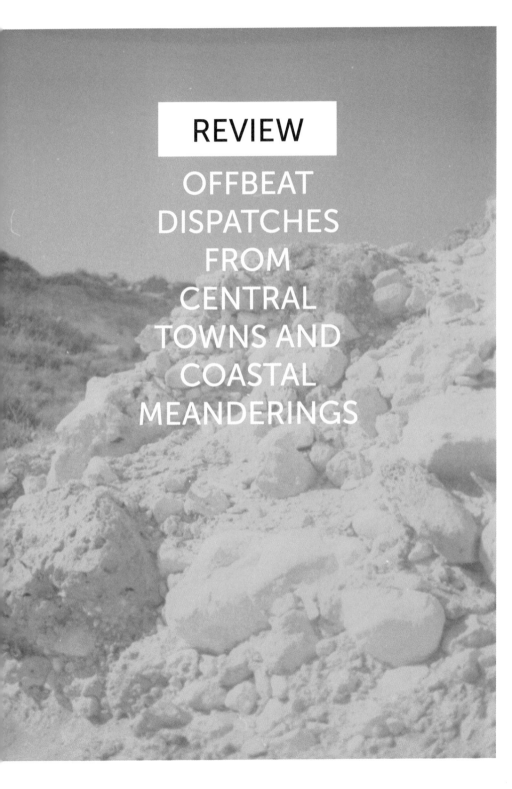

REVIEW

OFFBEAT
DISPATCHES
FROM
CENTRAL
TOWNS AND
COASTAL
MEANDERINGS

A STORY OF CARPEW

Slavko Vukanovic

The Fighting Kentuckian (1949) John Wayne, Vera Ralston.

Back then, in 1995, my homeland Serbia was in shambles. Brutal wars, sanctions and a collapse of economy made life very difficult for a 24 year old. Must I forever be a beggar, I thought. Would those golden dreams not come true?

Through my phone pal (long story), Spiridion Mangion, I managed to get a seven-day visa to Malta with a hope that I'll make use of a week's time and find a job as a waiter, dishwasher or anything else that would bring bread on the table.

Refusals lasted for five days until I got a trial with Żebbuġ Rangers Football Club. With some luck and five goals scored on that game, I appeared the next day in a newspaper as the newly signed player with Rangers. Yellow and green emblem sat nicely on my youthful chest. Few days later I moved to the centre of Żebbuġ. Very quickly I became known to locals as a popular striker, who followed my every step, making sure to tip off the club committee every time I bought a Cisk - the local beer.

Żebbuġ is quite a big village for Maltese standards and its centre hosts nine bars: three religious, two political, one football and three independent.

My instant choice was one of the independent ones, The Golden Lion, or as locals called it – The Carpew.

It was in the mid 80s when a great visionary, Paul Farrugia, had built this place. Paul was a great film lover who had a collection of 1,600 films on 35mm reel. His collection was mostly made up of films about cowboys and indians. He adored John Wayne. The upper floors of his house were invaded by the reels and different types of projectors. I'm not sure if his wife Mary appreciated this much. The first thing on entering Carpew are the tears. An overwhelming joy that a place like this exists. Carpew was a nexus of passion and business, fantasy and reality, half a petrol station, half a bar, half a billiard hall, half a body building shop.

People from Żebbuġ never liked Paul much, they believed he was spiking the petrol with water. Since his petrol station was the only one in Żebbuġ, they'd always come back for more, but most of them refused to have a drink at his bar or buy protein cans from Paul's son, Sandro. Apart, of course, from the few alchies, my first friends from Żebbuġ.

The bar occupied an area of no more than 12 square metres. In the centre, there was a large billiard table that made it difficult to approach the bar. Not Paul nor Sandro, nor much anybody else, was ever interested in playing pool but it always stood there, in spite of everything.

Two tables with three chairs each were placed on each side of the room. The wall was packed with framed photographs of Nazi soldiers with some WWII original letters from the front, written in German, along with a couple of small photos of Mussolini.

Behind the lime wooden bar, stood Mary, unsuccessfully trying to balance whispering and screaming at customers. On her left hand side, hanging tough, was a life-size poster of Sylvester Stallone and behind her, looming large, a poster of Ronald Reagan.

That was my place to rest, regroup and have a quiet drink.

As it happens, dear reader, in the late nineties, Paul had to sell his bar to a young chap who modernized it completely, bringing DJs and sexy girls. Exotic, enigmatic and magnificently chaotic, Carpew was too strange to survive the wave of new trends.

Paul and his wife moved to Arizona, in United States, where today he runs a drive-in cinema.

ACCIDENTAL PILGRIM'S LOG BOOK

Chris Bianchi

Latitude: 35.850168   Longitude: 14.416871

Latitude (DMS): 35°51'0.6048"N   Longitude (DMS): 14°25'0.7356"E

IS-SALIB TAL-GĦOLJA also known as Laferla Cross.
Erected on the highest hill in Malta, 27th September 1903.
Originally formed part of life size *Via Crucis*, an initiative of Fr. Paul Laferla of
Siġġiewi.
The cross, 16 metres high, iron and coated in bronze, was made at Pietrasanta in
Italy. It cost Lm800.00 (€1,863.50). A special government concession exempted
it from custom duty. This current cross is not the original, but a replacement. The
first being blown off by inclement weather in 1937.
Each year thousands make the pilgrimage up to the cross. At the base of it, they
leave their mark.

ARCHITECTURAL FOLLIES

Nicholas de Piro

photography

David Pisani

It is almost a miracle, a wonder, that considering the small size of the Maltese islands, they should contain so much architectural variety. There are the earliest free-standing constructions in the world; remains from early civilisations, then on to the Norman, the Gothic and the Baroque. Marvels were created in Malta in the 16th century including some of the finest fortifications anywhere for the 'new' city of Valletta. In spite of severe bombings all around, we can still look astonished at the glory of the Magisterial Palace of the Grand Masters and the incomparable almost reckless magnificence of the Conventual Church of St John.

Through the influence of the Knights of Malta and the Catholic Church and the developing sophistication of the local gentry, one finds a continuation of architectural creation with splendour into the 17th and 18th centuries. Perhaps it was due to the impact of a variety of styles that the 19th and early 20th century contrived a number of newer follies which continued to be peppered all over the little nation that is Malta. These pictures with their captions and commentaries should be considered partly as an anthropological study and also as a diversion – an entertainment. They illustrate and even illuminate the aspirations, ambitions, taste and often the confidence of the people of Malta.

If they are to be criticised perhaps for being elitist, then we should remember that they were created to delight. Like Malta's wonderful paintings, carvings, silver and lace, they were actually made by humble folk. They are not only a remarkable amount of evidence of talent and skill, but they are also a surviving monument to the very people who made them. It is right and fair that we should also remember those who inspired these constructions, those whose virtuosity has left us this legacy – a patrimony mostly happily appreciated, protected and enjoyed by one and all.

Stricter rules from the planning authorities are making follies more and more difficult to create. A modern way of life also does not lend itself well to the flamboyant self-indulgence which often characterises a folly. We must therefore protect and conserve what we have got, and hope that these precious and fanciful caprices are well identified and even affectionately preserved for everybody to enjoy.

Selmun Palace, Mellieħa

This is an outstanding 18th century folly. The late Leonard Mahoney author of '5000 Years of Architecture in Malta' says, "... Selmun Castle ... had the semblance, one imagines for romantic reasons, of the earlier fortified houses." It clearly has more flare than its grander sister Verdala Castle. The 'all-around' stone balcony is married in to the construction with apparent skill and taste. There is more of Louis Quinze here than there is of any seicento austerity.

The Gourgion Tower, Transfiguration Avenue, Lija

The Belvedere Tower was built for the 6th Baron of Budach Giuseppe de Piro Gourgion, 1845-1916, as the crowning glory to his magnificent garden in the village of Lija. It is round and there are four floors with, once upon a time, a wonderful view from the top, not only of the garden but much further afield, blocked only partially by the Parish Church. The architect employed was Giuseppe Bonavia, 1821-1885. He was the creator of a variety of most creditable works and even went to Venice for inspiration before designing his great facade for the Buttigieg-Francia Palace that was to face the Royal Opera House.

Casa Gourgion, Cathedral Square, Mdina

This is another of Giuseppe de Piro Gourgion's architectural follies. Clearly it was built to fascinate. Although so often criticised by the purists, it has embedded itself into the cultural psyche of most lovers of Mdina. I note that a good number of holiday snaps (as we used to say) use the Gothic House as background.

Nymphæum, Villa Bologna, Attard

Villa Bologna was built by the same architect who designed Selmun Palace. It was supposed to be 'splendid' – a riposte to one-and-all that the owner was able to endow his daughter with the finest of houses, and that she was eligible to marry into the nobility. The great nymphæum in the gardens is a folly to outstrip most other garden furnishings.

Casino dei Nobili aka Casino Notabile, Rabat

This charmingly Victorian, over-decorated, stately railway station club, created for members of the Maltese Nobility to meet in, now deserves 'unique' status and should be preserved as a curiosity; a little museum of Maltese aspiration in the 19th century. It was designed and built by Webster Paulson, 1837-1887, during the last year of his life.

Turkish Cemetery, Marsa

Emmanuele Luigi Galizia, 1830-1906, chief government architect, designed the Turkish Cemetery at Marsa. On a visit to Malta in 1867, the Sultan of Turkey, Abdul Aziz, presented Galizia with the Order of the Mejidie, and financed the building which was completed in 1874. For this commission Galizia based his design on Persian-Indian architecture.

Moorish Residential Follies, Rudolph Street, Sliema

Later, in a similar style, Galizia built himself a summer residence in Rudolph Street, Sliema, which he called Alhambra. He created three terraced houses, two of which of one storey, and the central one with two storeys – however, all together, they unite into an amalgamated unison.

Addolorata Cemetery, Paola

Should we also call this a folly? From the point of view of it being delicate and different it is certainly a poetic manner of introducing the outremonde in lacy, Gothic tracery on a usually baroque Malta. It is here that some think Emmanuele Luigi Galizia, 1830-1906, produced his masterpiece.

DAPPLES OF SENGLEA

Gordon Guillaumier

1. furbo - *streetwise local pup*
2. *sally under the archway*
3. dgħajsa - *the local gondola, no better way to see the grand harbour. call boatman tony +356 79492250*
4. *miracle statue, redeems every ailment*
5. senglea civitas invicta - *invincible city*
6. *sweet home*
7. fra claude de la sangle - *sacrae domus hospitalis sancti johannis hierosolymitani seu melitensis magnus magister*
8. madonna bambina - *the local protector*
9. *french creek emptied out*
10. *yellow giraffes*
11. *trapeze shape football field, minus one player for the team defending the narrowest side.*
12. *parish kitsch*
13. *rusty scroll*
14. *grand belvedere walkway... a gob smacking view!*
15. *st. michael about to massacre a demon*

16. *looking up*
17. *early morning* luzzu
18. *m.c. escher was also evidently spellbound by this place*
19. *senglea regatta club bar, nothing beats a sunset gin and tonic here*
20. l-isla, *regatta rowers*
21. *siren street*
22. *bastion shade*
23. *eye spy*
24. *cobbled passage way*
25. *watch out*
26. sanctum sanctorum
27. *after the bombing*
28. *ġnien il-gardjola*
29. *basking in the sun*
30. *bougainvillea*
31. *embracing rowers*
32. gallarija
33. *local trade*
34. *senglea gunners*
35. *gecko curtain call*

BIRŻEBBUĠA CONTAINED

Nina Gerada

Birżebbuġa is a seaside town that has been ruined in many ways, which is why few people would recommend you visit it.

It is for the same reason that this town is so interesting; this is where the island's dirty laundry hangs, revealing stories of war, colonisation and corruption, telling of a place that feels forgotten by its own country.

Give Birżebbuġa some attention and you will learn more about Maltese identity than in any other place.

The map outlines a rough route along the town's promenade, it is purposely fragmented, pointing out details and leaving others for you to discover. Use it to explore, it will reveal anecdotes and secrets. Wander off its proposed route and discover some for yourself…

Explore the area and look out for scars from every period in Maltese history; this area is rich in pre-historic settlements and Megalithic Temples. It was the first place to be inhabited by the Phoenicians, it houses the remains of a Roman Villa and is scattered with fortifications built by both the Knights of Saint John and the British during World War Two. More recently it has been heavily impacted by the large amount of industry thrown its way, and has seen a massive influx of asylum seekers due to the proximity of the Immigration Detention Facilities.

1. As you walk along the promenade keep an eye on the Freeport, a trans-shipment hub built in 1988, its large cranes cannot be missed. It is indisputably the landmark of the town, whether the inhabitants like it or not. The Freeport is quite a spectacle; dancing cranes, clumsy container liners turning in the bay, and the 'lego-land' repetitive patterns made by the piled up containers. It has an industrial beauty about it. Yet bear in mind that this has completely taken over every view from the town, it obscures the natural horizon, fills the bay with the echoing sound of clanking containers, and at night it floods it with yellow light. This heavy stamp of international shipping has marked Birżebbuġa and its inhabitants so deeply, yet none of these containers are destined for Malta, they stop here in transit. The Freeport seems a poignant reminder of Malta's relationship with the rest of the world: that of being a well positioned rock - a convenient harbour, an aircraft carrier and now a concrete strip on which to unload containers.

2. On a quiet summer's afternoon set up your umbrella in a dilapidated hotel (accessed from the St. George's Bay promenade). This used to be a wedding reception venue, which newlyweds would leave by boat, heading straight to Gozo for their honeymoon.

3. Swim in the shadow of the 18th century Ferretti battery.

4. Enjoy the rare moments when you can see the horizon.

5. Dream of ancient civilisations, investigate the deep wells and cart ruts cut into the limestone sea bed of Saint George's Bay. Is this where the name Birżebbuġa comes from? (Bir=well, żebbuġa=olive)

6. Wonder at the crazy juxtaposition of the large gas tanks towering behind pretty, little houses. These were originally built by British Petroleum and are now in use by Enemalta Corporation, Malta's main suppliers of electricity and gas.

7. On 2 December 1989, a few weeks after the fall of the Berlin wall, Bush and Gorbachev met in this bay for the Malta Summit, marking the end of Cold War hostilities. Malta was chosen for its strategic position in the Mediterranean, where East meets West and North meets South. They were set to meet aboard the American aircraft carrier, USS Belknap, but on the night in question, a violent north easterly storm blew into the protected harbour and Gorbachev cancelled the dinner, feeling uneasy about leaving his ship. So Bush joined Gorbachev for dinner aboard the soviet cruise ship Maxim Gorky, whilst the crew on board the American carrier were invited to enjoy the lavish meal that had been prepared for this momentous occasion. The summit thus became known as the 'seasick summit'.

8. Imagine what the town used to look like. Stop and admire the *villeġġjatura* (holiday homes) lining the seaside. Birżebbuġa was once a small settlement of these pretty, little two-storey houses. These *villeġġjatura* houses once existed all over the island's coastal towns but many have been demolished for the construction of flats or hotels. Take them in, who knows how much longer they will be here for.

9. Get political. Walk around the town's dilapidated water polo club. Ask a local how it ended up this way.

10. Kalafrana, where the Freeport now stands, used to be a British seaplane base, and so Birżebbuġa transformed into a strip full of the bars and entertainment facilities necessary to keep the officers happy. Look around town for the Lido Cinema and other remnants of this period.

11. Buy Malta's best fish and chips from Borda's and eat them on a bench by the sea.

12. Find the perfect fishing spot.

13. Listen to the dead silence during a Boċċi tournament on a summer's evening.

14. Sit by the salt pans and let the ground and walls reveal their stories to you. This area, known as Wied il-Buni, used to house two British gun posts, a large defence wall and moat. Part of the wall is visible behind the Boċċi Club and, if you study the ground closely, you can make out the footprints of the gun posts.

15. Drink a Cisk lager, eat some *hobż biż-żejt* (preferably sitting on a metal chair) and watch the cranes, containers and ships manoeuvring in and out of the Freeport.

SILENT CITY
KID - BURN
AND RUN

James Manduca

The citadel of Mdina was Malta's Capital until 1568. It is home to 300 citizens, and life here, they will tell you, is not without its eccentricities. Driving into the medieval, fortified city is forbidden unless you are a resident, provisions need to be sourced outside the walls, and opening a front door often brings close contact with the intrepid explorer holding up a camera.

As the daily throng of visitors arrive in the morning to visit the palaces, churches and museums, the residents are bustling around behind those walls, getting ready to exit the city, head to work and drop off the children at school. In the evening, as the crowds dwindle, they return to dine with their families around old tables under fusty chandeliers, the ancestral portraits looking down as they sup. When the silent city windows light up, one can truly sense the contemporary, private lives behind the timeless, public walls.

And as for the kids, they still enjoy a rare freedom. They run around the periphery walls and under the city, they know of invisible places. With its tight streets and secret nooks, Mdina is a wondrous labyrinth of hideouts and lairs. Indeed, all those who enter here can engage with this sense of playfulness and awe. Daybreak expeditions and night walking recommended.

Sunrise

Late night, long day, early morning.
Whether up really early before a fishing trip, whether coming home after a late night out, whether you're taking a 5 am walk after a long night of deadlines, or whether you lose track of time in good company, 'the bastions' is the place to be when the sun is rising.

Festa Race Track

Also doubles up as the 'main street' of Mdina. The neat lines of people lining it on festa night, together with flag-poles, banners, hanging light bulbs and finish line transform this street into an Olympic-style race track for just one night of the year.

Local Football Pitch

This is where 'Mdina rules' football is played. Rules su as the 'mini-nies' rule and the 'five stone-slab' distan for free-kicks are practised here (with, might I a the blessing of the previous Archbishop, who wou occasionally join in, just to see the smiles on our face

Secret Tunnel

This is one of many tunnels in and around Mdina, the exact location of which is in fact... secret.

Closed-Off Walkway

Part of a stretch of garden/platfo running along a line of fortificatio

Roller-Hockey Arena

Broomsticks, planks of wood, w wood glue, rollerblades and a ten ball – an enterprising recipe for a f afternoon and a couple of brui too.

Secret Garden

Part of the same stretch of fortifications. (Also part of the 'adventure' label!)

Underground Party Zone

This is where parties have changed over the years, but still always boil down to meeting up with your friends, who are more like your family, and having a good time.

Adventure

Skip, jump, run, climb, balance, f adventure...

Burn & Run

Right at the climax of summer, the Mdina festa falls on the third weekend of July.

It's summer, and you know it's summer. If the forty-degree heat and late evening light don't give it away, the fireworks (21 gun salute to the season) will be sure to shake you out of the lull that comes over on returning home after a day at the beach. The barrage of petards lets you know that it's your favourite season. You're on your way home with calm and contented eyes/eyes full of salt water/chlorine and your cheeks are glowing like the houses in the early evening sun. But you know that today is festa night, it's almost like a sixth sense, a special kind of feeling.

After getting ready, you hurry out of the house and start making your way, your pace quickened by the beat *tal-banda*. You're running now, as fast as you can, to your friend's house, hoping that he'll hear the frantic knocking and ringing of doorbells over the sea of trumpets and trombones. Finally, someone opens the door and you rush up to the second floor balcony where your sole mission is to land a scrunched up ball of shredded papers right in the mouth of the tuba! The adults sprinkle a light mist of shredded papers, you and your friends have a more important task; with an implacable gaze fixed directly on the tuba, you go about your mission with steadfast determination.

The band passes by and you rush back outside, onto the streets where you work in teams, collecting papers into neatly collected piles at any available corner of the street. Of course, there is always some competition from even younger and smaller groups of children, but they soon loose heart when they see your mountains of paper collected with efficiency that would put a Mercedes production line to shame. With that sorted, you can now focus on the next event – the festa races. The fear is that the not-so-accurate organiser's watch will strike 10 p.m. before you arrive at the starting line on Main Street. You get there early. First race is for toddlers, they waddle down the road, cheered on by doting onlookers. The one who wins this one is usually the slightly older-looking one whose qualification for this particular race baffles many (but not everyone).

Of the four age (rather height) categories of 'athletes' races, the most intense one is always last. With the 'young adolescent to fully grown' men category, the race has a fierce intensity. When the finish line is moved back, all the way to the door of the Carmelite Church, you know they mean business. After two false starts, the third false start is unanimously declared good. The scene that ensues is more akin to the running of the bull, or wildebeest stampede through the streets of Mdina.

THREE!, TWO!... GO! Wait, what happened to one? No time to argue, you need to catch up with the bastard who held you back at the start line and used you as a push-off to propel himself into the lead. This fuels you to go faster. You're flying now, if only you could see yourself. You have just gone into hyper-drive and the world around is a blur of unmixed streaks of colour. One or two faces seem to defy the laws of nature and are in perfect and crisp focus – their wide-eyed expression and open mouth cheer you on. More than a sprint this is a race of hurdles. But you mustn't be distracted, it's a minefield out there... `Jutting-out prams and renegade toddlers are worrying but it's the 'gambetta', the leg that shoots out to make you stumble that you really have to look for, you're never expecting those.

You never realise how long the street really is until the last twenty metres or so when it curls ever so slightly uphill. Finally, the sight of two tall poles, decorated with modest prizes all the way to the top, demark the finish line. If you are lucky enough to come in first, you get first choice from the twin towers of prizes. If second or third, you hope, against all hope, that the *palju* isn't chosen before it's your turn to pick a prize. The *palju* or hand-held fan is the only semi-decent prize on there, but even if you don't get to pick the *palju* you learn to stay away from any plastic prizes... you go for a t-shirt instead.

Amidst pats of congratulations on the back and 'I didn't know you could run so fast!'s you make your way, red in the face and with eyes still slightly restless from the race, to the square, to await the culmination of the entire night – the ground fireworks display. You notice that amongst the familiar rickety firework stands, handmade, sticking out of gauged out holes in the ground, there is a new, daring-looking one. You wonder what a 'safe' distance to stand from the fireworks would be, and whether to give in to bravado.

All eyes are on the fireworks now and the glowing amber at the end of the stick is being taken closer to the edge of the (almost) circular firework wheel. There is a silence just at the moment before the amber ignites the first firework with a fizzling sound. As the wheel starts turning, the stand starts shaking, then the rest of the wheels on the stand start to ignite and a shower of bright droplets of light are sent spinning off the sides of the wheels in a steady flow.

You look at either side of the firework, scouting for any bystanders who might be in range when the firework eventually goes out with a bang. The red embroidered material draped out of the windows on either side of the firework is also cause for concern (a slightly excited one). The cloud of sulphur that comes off the fireworks fills your eyes; the smell a catalyst for memories to come. The final firework – the 'VSE' (Viva Sant' Elia), signals the end of the night for most, and with a final applause the crowd starts to diffuse until it's just you and your friends left in an empty pjazza, under the skeletons of the burnt-out fireworks. You and your friends anxiously wait, until there's nothing but the tumbleweed of shredded paper blowing across the square. Once the coast is clear, your efforts then return to the mountains of shredded paper that you had meticulously and efficiently gathered earlier on. And just like that, festa night turns into bonfire night.

Mdina Cathedral

BEHIND CLOSED SHUTTERS

Franziska
von Stenglin

Stone, dog; Tarxien

Glass, wood; Attard

Ceramic, glass, painted tiles; Ta' Xbiex

Porcelain, wood, cloth, straw, gold, silver, pearls, sunglasses; Żejtun

Porcelain, wood, cloth; Lija

Wood, glass, ceramic, light bulb; Attard

Marble, stone; Vallett

Crystal, gold, wood, glass Blata I-Bajda

Images taken from the Project 'The Rock from Underneath' (2009)

ST. THOMAS'
TRAIL

Sandra Banthorpe

Field notes:

St. Thomas Bay is: a village/ settlement/ hamlet/ community/ precinct/ township/ burg/ municipality.

It lies on the edge of Marsascala, not far from Żejtun
Marsascala - a fishing village that developed into a town, it surrounds the neighbouring bay.

It's a little like the wild west; inhabited boat houses, trailers and caravans.
The first few boat houses were built in the 1950s; they were used in the summer months by families from 'the three cities', which is the area of Cottonera, located around the Grand Harbour creeks.

Growth of the *villeġġjatura* has been slow, with little outside influence.
It is a place where necessity is the mother of all invention, teeming in the summer and haunting in the winter.

Swimming is possible all year round. In the summer families on the sand, tanned kids on the rocks, looking for shade from the low, smooth cliffs. In winter it is sheltered and the sea is shallow, warm, enjoyed by the elderly, pale-skinned visitors, hardy eastern European men and brave locals.

In the time of the Knights, Ottoman and Barbary pirates used to land in Marsascala to take water and/or to seek refuge from the rough seas, usually causing havoc by stealing, and harassing/kidnapping the locals.

Often, the elderly and women and children would be rushed up to Żejtun or Żabbar by their men folk when sightings were made. It is recorded that in July, 1614, a 60-strong fleet of Turkish vessels, loaded with marauders tried to make a shock landing at Marsascala, but the hardy Maltese gave them battle and drove them away in a humiliating defeat.

SO I NEED A HOE

Nick Tabone
photography
Jon Banthorpe

Let me explain. I've only been in Malta a week, but I've landed on my feet. I'm staying in a family friend's place in Lija - a perfect location as the village is located pretty much smack dab in the centre of Malta. Real character this house and gee whiz what a garden. There are orange and lemon trees, pomegranate, grapefruit and olive too. Thing is, the garden, like the house, hasn't been touched in two years, and one of the conditions of my staying here is that I'll do a little fixing up both inside and outside.

I came here for a wedding but I'm thinking I'll try and find some work, maybe in the movies. Any excuse to stay for the summer. Maltese summers are the best and I've not had one in a while. I've just spent the winter living and working on a Tall Ship in Lunenberg, Nova Scotia[1]. It is a small fishing village on the south shore of Eastern Canada, settled originally by the British and populated mostly by Swiss and German immigrants in the last hundred years. It is beautiful, a UNESCO town of heritage, but totally dead that time of year. I figured a wedding was a good excuse to come out. It's June. The sea is the best temperature around this time and from Lija I'm no more than a fifteen-minute drive to some of my favourite swimming spots (Peter's Pool and Żurrieq). Did I mention I'm supposed to DJ at this wedding? I'm a little worried about it 'cos truth be told, I'm not a very good DJ.

I always feel a little anxious when about to perform any kind of transaction here. Despite the fact that I'm a 'halfie'[2] and have spent at least five (not all at once)

1   Nova Scotia is one of Canada's Maritime provinces
2   A 'halfie' is someone who is half Maltese. In my case my father is Maltese,
my mother is British and somehow I ended up Canadian.

of my 34 years on this island, I still feel very much a foreigner, and therefore at the mercy of any shop clerk. Customer service is a crap shoot in Malta and one seems to only ever experience each end of the spectrum from phenomenally rude to genuinely kind and helpful. Today I figure I'll go to the ironmonger round the corner from where my folks live in St.Julian's. Only 'cos I know it's there and that I'll be able to park. I run upstairs to their flat, ostensibly to say hi to them, but mostly say hi to Pippa their ungainly tal-kaċċa dog[3]. When I open the door she is there waiting and she emits a drawn out high pitch whine, which is her declaration of love as she paws and licks and jumps at me. She always makes me feel better about myself. I've only been here six days so my parents are still happy to see me. This will wear off in time. I tell my dad about my mission and he tells me the guy at the ironmonger is very helpful. This is good news. I leave and head down the hill.

There is something about Maltese pavements. It sometimes seems that they're composed of mostly glycerine because I always slip on them. Today I'm wearing a pair of flip flops that I haven't really had a chance to break in. They're O'Neills. I got them in St. Barth's two winters ago after my old pair blew out in Antigua. The old ones were great. Comfortable, good tread, nary a blister in three years. These new ones are useless. There is no tread on their soles! What was I thinking when I forked out 40 Euros for them!

Normally, I'm a very fast walker, irritatingly fast most of my friends will tell you, but today I'm taking half steps to avoid wiping out. This is making me even more nervous. I cross Mrabat street at the zebra crossing. In Malta you really need to assert your right as a pedestrian and sometimes that means stepping out into traffic, 'cos you know, if you wait for someone to stop for you it could be Christmas by the time they actually do. Some guy in a red escort slams on his brakes and yells something at me in Maltese. I don't speak Maltese but I understand what he says well enough and it's not nice. I walk with my eyes on the ground, this is partially to avoid any dog turds, but also to keep from making eye contact with anyone passing by, a big city tactic that I seem to take with me everywhere. I like my anonymity, especially when I've built up an adequate steam of anxiety, and in Malta it's so easy to bump into someone you know, a good thing, but today the prospect of making small talk with someone I haven't seen in years gives me the heebie-jeebies. I turn the corner onto Old College Street.

I slip.

I go down backwards but my reflexes are good today. My hands go out behind me and break my fall, and in a manoeuvre that would have made James Brown proud, I spring back upright, as if I almost meant to do it. Still, my face flushes with embarrassment but the good news is, I'm pretty much here. Alldecor Ironmonger.

In Canada hardware stores are vast, supermarket sized buildings with aisle upon aisle of tools, sports gear, automotive equipment and even kitchen ware. They are staffed by a giant, generally red-shirted, super-smiley bunch of people who are ultra-knowledgeable about their products and where they are located. Conversely here, the average hardware store is tiny and mostly staffed by a single person behind a counter. But what is truly extraordinary is how they

3   Tal-Kaċċa are a local breed of hunting dog.

manage to conjure anything you ask for out of seemingly nowhere, like the whole place were some kind of magician's hat. I enter the store. There are three people in the queue in front of me. This could take a while.

I take the time to make a mental tally of just what it is I want. There's just one guy in front now. He's talking to the dude behind the counter. Maltese. I pick out words here and there. Xemx. Xita. Arsenal[4]. A few more minutes drift by. The guy takes a paper bag with some nuts and bolts in it, pays and leaves. My turn.

My dad was right. The guy is super-helpful. I explain to him where I'm living and what I imagine I will be doing. Turning the soil. Cutting back. Weeding. He doesn't understand 'hoe' and I don't know the Maltese word. I do my best mime. Hands together behind my back, swing and presto. He smiles reaches behind a curtain and produces a hoe. He even recommends a few things I hadn't thought of buying. This is what I leave the place with:

1 x spade
1 x pair gardening gloves
1x pair shelf brackets
1 x pruning scissors
1 x well bucket (There's a well in the garden!)
1 x hoe
My work here is done.

So that was all six months ago. I'm still here and I'm still living in the house in Lija. Anthony Burgess once lived in this village. He writes about it in the opening chapter of Earthly Powers. I did get work in the movies and I did DJ at that wedding and you know what, I wasn't too bad.

And the house...

The house has been great. As I said earlier the place is old. 1797 it says on the lintel above the garden door. That's almost as old as Canada. It is a single-storey building situated off a quiet, little alley. It has very high ceilings and a large living area in the front. The central courtyard has a separate building off it which has another bedroom and bathroom. And then there's the garden. It is cruciform in shape. There is an arched pathway covered in vines which leads to the bottom, a small fountain to the right and trees and plants all about. The garden walls are high and shrouded in Bougainvillea. Many of my friends here have helped me. One hot summer day J, E and H showed up and whilst J replaced the exterior plumbing, the rest of us got our hands dirty in the garden and at the end of the day we celebrated with Pimms and lemonade in the courtyard. This gave me tremendous satisfaction - for the last ten years or so I have been mostly transient. Kind of like the devil in Job who when asked by God where he's been all these years replies: 'I've been travelling to and fro in the world and moving up and down in it.' But it's in this house that I've found the closest thing to a home in all this time, and despite the lack of my own material possessions within it, and the obvious fact that I don't own it, it has, for however fleeting a moment, become my space. My home. A place where friends can come over, proffer advice on the garden, lend a hand, or simply see out the day with a glass of Pimms or a Cisk[5] in their hand. I often think how great it would be if any of my friends from home came for a visit. To the average Canadian this kind of place just isn't on the radar. I would love for them to come and see it. Let them in on my Maltese life and into my secret Maltese garden.

It has been a learning curve. This isn't like any house I've lived in before and there are a few things you should and shouldn't do in old Maltese houses. Rule #1 - Don't slam doors because a) the door might fall off or b) a piece of the ceiling or wall may come away and kill you. Rule #2 - Forget everything you know about windows and breezes. Maltese windows must be left shuttered in the summer if you want the place to remain cool and dust free. Rule #3 - I don't want to sound like a hippy, but sometimes you need to take a deep breath, sit down, and appreciate the peculiar things life throws your way. Rule #4 - Don't walk naked around rose bushes. Life lessons these.

And what about that hoe?

Well, I hoed. And I dug. And I cut. And I'm still doing it. I have a helper here now. His name is Bruce. He is an abandoned Chihuahua, locally called a pocket dog, tal-but. I found him at the film studios, he's the ugliest thing you've ever seen, but he's quiet and he's charming in his own way, and he follows me around as I work in the garden with a forlorn expression on his snaggle-toothed face, showing his approval by peeing here and there.

The thought of me reinventing myself in my thirties as some kind of idiot-savant gardener is a strange one. I've never had any great affinity to plants and I've always despised insects. Not all of them, just the ones that go buzz. According to Tabone family legend, when I was a toddler and we lived on Broadway Avenue in Toronto, there was a sand-box out back. In the summer I would go out to play in it with a bucket and spade wearing my underpants, wellington boots and a balaclava, the latter worn to muffle their buzzing. And as for my gardening knowledge, just a couple of weeks back E came round again and took a look at the garden. I was showing her the weeds I've been ripping up with extreme prejudice since I got here. She looked at one of them and informed me it was a tenacious plant that would eventually produce a lovely flower. You can't win 'em all I guess. So it goes.

Oh, did I mention what happened when I left the Ironmonger. I stepped out the door and slipped on the sidewalk. This time my hands were full. I went down like the trade centre, tools all over the pavement. A car nearby honked its horn. I looked up from the ground and there was someone I didn't know inside it smiling at me. Apparently he thought it so funny he had to let me know. Even I had to laugh at that one.

---

5   *Cisk is the Maltese lager. It is amazing!*

(DON'T) GO TO HAMRUN

photography
Sandra Banthorpe

It's always hectic in Hamrun. It got so bad they built a bypass, so you could bypass Hamrun. The main road is still the artery between Birkirkara and Valletta, here the car invariably slips into second gear and you find yourself stuck behind a bus, with no chance of overtaking. Consider this lucky, you can hang an arm out of the car and almost touch the façades of the shops, bars, fast food joints, the football club, the band club, the church steps. Blast techno if you want to blend in.

Take your pick: Maxim's pastizzi for a fast snack; Liverpool Bar for a game of pool and a bottle of Cisk. There's a tailor, a clock trove, a resilient sweet shop. They'll be quick to make you feel at home. There's always time to stop and say hello, time to linger a while if you're not double-parked and waiting for a pizza. Walk in any direction you like, then cross the street and walk back. Along the way look out for C&M Borg Coffee Service. It always smells so good. Rico is the house blend, which you can use to percolate. Here, you can pick up the Maltese blend. The traditional way to make coffee in Malta is a dying art. But it is not dead. You can still drink it at Tas-Sidor, also called Café du Paris, in the nearby town of Qormi. Maltese coffee is cooked the Turkish way. It is flavoured with chickpeas, cloves and aniseed. When cooking it add tangerine or orange peel. Less seasonal and more perfumed is the orange blossom water, (*ilma żahar*); add a few drops when cooking.

Easy to spot are the men weaving baskets, cane shades and man fans. The shades can be seen all over Malta, in front of doors or draped over balconies to provide respite from the harsh sun, to stop paint from fading. If you want one, order a *hasira*. The soft baskets are perfect for carrying vegetables and beach towels. If you want one of these order a *ġewlaq*. The brilliant man fan goes by the name of *palju*.

Other useful words in Hamrun are San Gejtanu and Spartans. Each word arouses great passion and devotion. Internal band club rivalry best viewed on the 7th of August during the parish feast.

When you are about to exit the town, turn back for one last glimpse and remember the 1st Hamrun Scout Group Duke of Argyll's Own motto: Forward Hamrun! _EM_

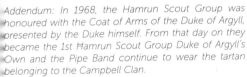

Addendum: In 1968, the Hamrun Scout Group was honoured with the Coat of Arms of the Duke of Argyll, presented by the Duke himself. From that day on they became the 1st Hamrun Scout Group Duke of Argyll's Own and the Pipe Band continue to wear the tartan belonging to the Campbell Clan.

FROM HAMRUN TO MARSAXLOKK IN FOUR HOURS

Alex Vella Gera

I was once on a bus in Msida when I overheard a Russian man ask somebody what was the name of this district of Valletta we were travelling through. I smiled knowingly because he had a point. From Żabbar to Attard, Valletta to Tarxien, one could easily consider the urban sprawl one single city occupying 15 to 20% of Malta's total area.

Right at the edge of Hamrun, where this urban sprawl takes a breather and allows some open space to dominate the landscape, lies a forgotten road. This dead stretch of tarmac [fig 1] tapering to a dead end was once a main road along which, for eleven long years, my school van zipped through traffic on its way to Cottonera. I remember it well, the free flow of cars where now there are none. Its function has been usurped by the complex of bypasses that were built in the early nineties to deal with congestion caused by the ever-increasing amount of cars on our roads.

I decide to start my aimless walk from this spot because it symbolises something I can't put my finger on. More than a symbol, this dead road incarnates a feeling, a sense of belonging, to what does not exist anymore; my past, my childhood, the world as it was then. This is not nostalgia but rather the opposite: recognition of a simple truth. Dead roads lead nowhere. They force me to improvise, to make do with what I've got at hand and put aside forever the romantic delusions that brought me to mull over this spot in the first place.

Indeed, the only way forward is down the steps leading to the tunnel that takes you under the bypass and out the other end. In such a no-man's land, bang in the middle of car territory, one is immediately forced to come to terms with the first rule of aimless walking in Malta. 'Main roads' have a gravitational pull, and no matter how you try to avoid them, and keep to the narrow, quiet, residential streets, at some point you're going to find yourself on the bank of another of those impassable rivers of traffic.

The tunnel beneath the bypass leads to a quaint, residential street where the sound of chirping birds manages to drown out the rumble of the morning traffic, still dangerously close behind. The contrast is breathtaking. Down this street I walk. It seems promising and I am happy to be on my way to who knows where, but, as suspected, the joy does not last. At a junction where a small bridge spans the concrete canal, constructed some years ago to deal with the flood waters which plague this area, I witness three separate instances of dogs pulling at their leash and dragging their owner with them. Like all good walkers, I am superstitious. This may mean something, I tell myself.

I enter the village streets of Qormi [fig 2]. The smell of baking bread hangs heavy at every street corner. A housewife's life in 2011 in this neck of the woods is still recognisable to her ancestors. I come across a market close to the church dedicated to Saint Sebastian. One of Qormi's two parishes, you can tell it's a comparatively new edifice (built in the 1980s) because it is at the edge of town and not right in its heart. A stone's throw away, another main thoroughfare holds sway, and after crossing it I find myself in trouble.

fig 2

fig 3

The only way ahead is along a typically uninviting stretch of road *[fig 3]*; a sign informs me that this leads to the airport. That direction does not suit my mood, so the only choice I have, outside of retracing my steps (never!), is walking on and hoping to find a turning into quieter territory. Sure enough, not more than a hundred paces farther along, just such an opportunity presents itself. I take it gladly, but before long find I am going round in circles. The gravitational pull of that main road leading to the airport is hard to break free from, and all streets to its side seem to lead back to it at some point, so much so that the flood water canal - practically bone dry - which I'd passed by earlier on, offers a fortuitous escape from this vicious circle.

I feel a rare sense of freedom as I follow it straight out of Qormi, past the Marsa race and golf courses. Perhaps I am in tune with some subliminal sense of the potential rainwater's passage, dragging me along in that dream-state common to walkers hypnotised by their own rhythm. Whatever it is, the canal leads me all the way to the other end of Marsa, to the Matthew Micallef St. John Athletic Stadium, named after a local athlete whose young life was cut short in a terrible traffic accident, whom I knew personally. I sit for a while in hazy contemplation, watching clueless school children attempting the high jump *[fig 4]*.

fig 4

fig 5

Albert Town is notorious, unfortunately, for its poor environmental stats (terrible air pollution) and social problems (prostitution, migrant centre) but to me it is simply a stepping stone between Marsa and the Addolorata cemetery, where there are probably more people buried than the whole living population of the archipelago. Apart from being the final resting place for most Maltese, the Addolorata cemetery is also a pleasant oasis of calm, especially at the far end, from where, after following a path circumventing the cemetery's outer perimeter *[fig 5]*, a melancholy path strewn with discarded bouquets and used up candles, I finally reach a dead end and have no choice but to climb over the cemetery wall to get in. I immediately find myself in a forgotten corner of the cemetery, that I discover to be the old burial area for stillborn babies. On marble slabs identical dates of birth and death stare back at me. I feel nothing.

Leaving the cemetery (this time through the front gate) I now cross over into the grid-like streets of Paola (*Raħal Ġdid* or New Town), which aside from being long and relatively calm, offer promising views into people's homes, owing to the good number of women who choose today to spring clean. I march on, sneaking peaks inside; the marble staircases, the kitsch statue in the entrance hallway, the smell of disinfectant taking me back across a lifetime of memories.

Up the hill I walk, following the straightest street I've encountered so far, all the way to the centre of Raħal Ġdid and further on, beyond the church, I press on sensing that I am approaching the edge of something.

It is a fact that an account of a walk through Malta could easily turn into a chronicle of visits to places in a state of abandon; some kind of waster's pilgrimage. For instance, the Corradino football stadium *[fig 6]* in which dereliction I bask for a moment's reverie before journeying on.

fig 6

These Maltese towns, whose topographical autonomy has long been swallowed up by the unending building development of the past thirty years, are hard to tell apart. Where does one end and another begin? Indeed, at one point I think I am still in Raħal Ġdid but have walked into Tarxien. This observation would not mean much if it wasn't for the fact that suddenly, without warning, I find myself in open countryside, the final, newly-built homes at the edge of Tarxien falling away behind me. So there it is, I've made it. I've managed to identify the very edge of this undefined, unnameable city.

The open country road leads me into idyllic scenery. The smell of manure now replaces that of car exhaust. I hear pigs, squealing as if in extreme agony. Is it slaughter day on the farm or is that how pigs always sound? Far ahead of me the church of Żejtun rises up, beckoning me towards her. I walk, head in the clouds, feeling my spirits rise. Soon enough I enter Żejtun. Passing a school I overhear unruly girls in a classroom. Żejtun's old streets wrap themselves around me, offering comfort which although welcome, is not enough to make me stop, for I can now sense my final destination. It has begun to reveal itself to me and what had started out as an aimless walk is now the opposite. I have an aim, I have a desire, to see the sea. To reach it on foot and to stand at the water's edge and feel I have accomplished something.

Crossing the whole length of Żejtun, for the first time on my journey I now start to look out for street signs: ones saying Marsaxlokk. I find a number of them, each one sending me dutifully to the next one, their arrows like villagers' fingers eager to help a stranger. With my legs tiring and gently aching I press on, happy to be at the end of my journey, soon to sit down in one of Marsaxlokk's famed fish restaurants and eat a hearty meal.

Finally, beyond a turning on the main road forming the perimeter of Żejtun, there it is, the only wide expanse of space available to the Maltese eye: the sea *[fig 7]*. I hurry on down the road then take a right turn down a country lane. Cars are few now, as I pass by the areas of Xrobb l-Għaġin and Tas-Silġ, where roadside chapels and villas coexist, as the road slopes downwards towards Marsaxlokk and the sea.

So ends a relatively short and simple walk (by most rambling standards), but an epic one nonetheless, because in its innocuous normality I'm sure there lies a hidden truth. Again, for the second time today, I can't put my finger on what is moving me. Perhaps it is nothing more than truth, the truth of being alive in the here and now, a state of mind that an aimless walk such as this one celebrates to the full.

g 7

THROUGH THE LOOKING GLASS

Elise Billiard

My name is Elise. But here they call me Alice.
I am not Maltese nor am I British or Italian. I am an outsider looking in.
I do not particularly like these Islands. I do not want to like them. The reason
why I remain here year after year...?

People say: Hi, How are you?
And then they leave me walk my way.
I walk through the lit streets, I walk through the dirty paths, I walk through the
islands, and along the cliffs. I look at the sea horizon. I never go in and on the
sea. I am on the island.
I look at the world from the island.
And the world looks new and full of beauties from here.

I came here by chance.
I don't travel much since I landed here. I might be trapped. I travel within the
island's limits, it's enough, I do not try to escape anymore.

Here people say: the world is small.
Maybe,
But from here you can see the whole world.

1. *Argotti gardens*
The inverted garden

2. *Ballade*
Seeking the Wild West

3. *Manderaġġio*
Hotel Manderaġġio

4. *Manuel's*
Next to Mellieħa cemetery

Valletta – mars 2008

5. Valletta, Mars 2008
The fisherman's dream

6. Door
After the party

Dingli cliff – mars 08

7. Dingli Cliffs
Where the light comes from

A VALLETTA VIEW

Wioletta Kulewska

Every night as I drift to sleep I see an octopus tentacle-tower waving goodnight through my bedroom window. It is the St Paul's Pro-Cathedral spire.

Soon I find my way to the imaginarium; a place to house the collection of the stone architectural shapes I see through my windows. And all around is the light, creamy colour of rock and the blue of the sea.

Every other window in Valletta is a portal for a new image, a new story and relationship.

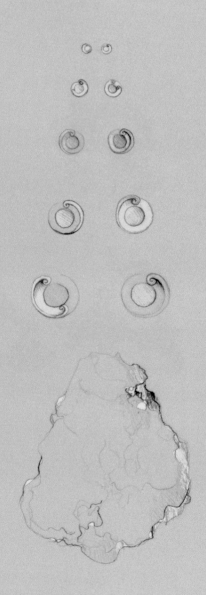

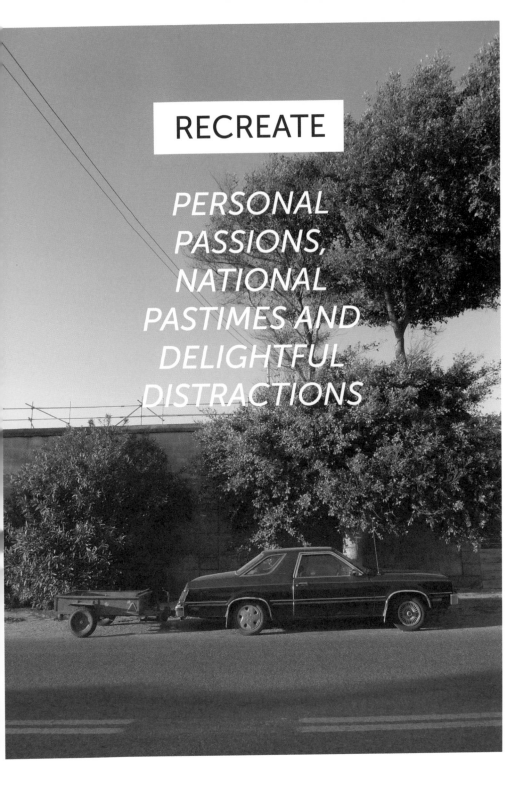

RECREATE

PERSONAL PASSIONS, NATIONAL PASTIMES AND DELIGHTFUL DISTRACTIONS

WE ARE ROCKS

Edward Said

HEATWAVE

Kurt Arrigo

ASPHALT OBSESSION & THE CULTURE OF NOISE

Joshua de Giorgio
photography
Jon Banthorpe

Asphalt: that mix of aggregate and viscous petroleum by-product. In its most mundane, functional interpretation, it represents a simple means of handling automotive transport, to others it symbolises the very pathway to vehicular transcendence. Now at first glance, it might seem that asphalt is something we have not fully mastered on this island, the roads being at best somewhat lumpy and uneven, and in many cases an exercise in suspension trashing. Yet weather permitting, on any given weekend, somewhere on an asphalted stretch on the island, someone out there is getting their kicks racing cars. Though there are no bespoke racetracks, the Maltese innate ability to adapt and make do means that any road with interesting enough corners or long enough straights is fair game. This is not only an observation on the local infrastructure but also perhaps an insight into the hands-on boffin attitude of the Maltese, and a measure of how single-mindedly *deliżżji* (hobbies) are pursued locally. Further to this, aural qualities of automotive racing and the culture it perpetuates appear to seamlessly coalesce in the islands other popular obsessions, which somehow tend to be fairly noisy affairs.

Like many things on these islands, the local obsession with all things automotive forms part of our colonial heritage. Many of the organisations that run automotive events are the direct spawn of, or at least tangentially related to, the British Forces, who were based on the islands until 1979. It is interesting that this is so, because drag racing is only really possible in Malta because of the decommissioned WWII runways that became available. One such runway, Hal-Far, is the local mecca for all those that wish to pit their reaction time and their mechanics ability to squeeze every last screeching horsepower out of

engines, against their peers. These events are perhaps the most extreme you will encounter locally, with everything from moderately tuned road cars, to ethanol burning custom-builds tearing down the runway in that perennial chase for faster times.

The scent of drying fennel, the warm breeze carrying the faintest whiff of ocean spray, the thunderous roar of a badly muffled, turbo charged beast; a bizarre contrast perhaps, but as the summer ends - or conversely begins - the hilly segments of our picturesque, often secluded, coastline hosts the diverse, bewildering crowd that is the Hillclimbing community. Hillclimbing is a different beast altogether. Perhaps one of the oldest forms of motor sport to still be practised, it enjoys a rabid, enthusiastic support locally. The concept is simple; organize participants into groups based on the relative power and level of modification of their cars, get some timing equipment and let them loose on the battered asphalt. The most popular from both driver and spectator's perspective are the fast, curvy tracks of Penellu in Mellieħa and the recently refurbished Mtaħleb venue. The cars themselves vary immensely, from fairly standard family saloons of the novice, the Japanese 4-wheel drive rally specials and arguably culminating at the motorbike-engined single seat vehicles.

Sporting details aside, it is not simply the competitive aspect of motor-sport which is interesting, rather it is the subculture that it creates, and has been so widely embraced on the islands. The car as an item of material culture is a complex one. Not only is it functional, in that it is a mode of personal transport, but as an object, it comes heavily loaded with social meaning. Perhaps once that material function of a car changes, in sport cars for example, these reflected

social values get somewhat obscured and twisted, but may still be discernible in a more subtle way. Evidence of this can be seen in the anachronistic nationalism-by-proxy of the Italy versus England camp that forms part of the racing psyche. Also, it is the way that perhaps these gatherings of men and their machines (for it is men, with few exceptions) seem to mimic so many other aspects of local gatherings. As individual cultural elements, the gaudy chromatic vibrancy, the sheer noise and apparent chaos and the ubiquitous fast food, could easily describe a village festa or political rally. This fascination with noise is perhaps the most glaringly obvious commonality here. Where the village feast is dominated by the viciously unpredictable barrages of the fireworks, the at times pleasingly familiar marching bands and more recently the relentless pounding of modern commercial dance music, these automotive gatherings bring to the general cacophony an orchestra of infernal mechanical rumblings. The crowd seems to revel in the screeching of rubber on the poorly surfaced road, the torturous wail of the engine straining against its mountings and the whoosh of the turbo dumping its excess gas. This unbridled enthusiasm for automotive noise also graces our public roads and spaces via the Boyracer community who bring another element to the mix, the in-car portable disco. Automotive racing and car culture are certainly not a singularly Maltese pastime, but somehow through a process of acculturation, they have taken on a very local flavour. The sheer energy and time people put into the cars and the events supersedes any physical limitations posed by lack of facilities. In their own way, they blend into the general background noise of the festa, the shrieking fish hawker or just the loud babble of local conversation, thus contributing to the island's unique, and at times unnerving, soundtrack.

THE BOYS ARE RACING

Sacha Maric

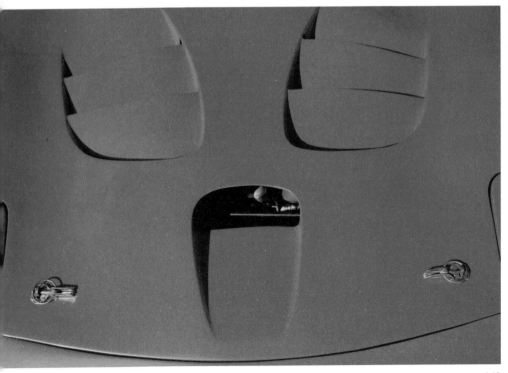

DAY AT THE RACES

Amelia Troubridge

THE MED DEVILS

Illustration
Harry Malt

Manchester United Supporters Club, Malta: a large white room, 1 giant screen, 3 TVs. You need them for when it gets rammed in here. It's raining tonight, so the place isn't packed. But it's busy with stout men and a few wives. Non-members pay €2.50, and there's a raffle so you can win a t-shirt, a white one. Nothing special. Cisk is €1.50 a bottle at the McFergie bar. If you want official merchandise you can get it in the souvenir cubicle.

Established in '59, the club is proud of its history and close ties with the Red Devils. The oldest overseas Man United Supporters Club, is what they'll tell you, they've all been here, many times - Ferguson, Scholes, Giggs, Neville. Beckham too, before he was a star.

An enormous black and white photograph of the fated 1958 Busby Babes spans a wall, the end of a dream is written in bold letters above it. Hand on your heart.

It's 20:30, the match begins and short men line up along the back of the block of chairs - the giant screen nice and low, they prefer to stand. Good viewing, great sound. All confident that Manchester United'll give Blackpool a good thrashing. But by half time there is only hushed blasphemy at the McFergie bar counter, with two goals for Blackpool and none for Man United; you can hear the crackle of crisp packets, the flicking of lighters at the window. Everyone's thinking about Charlie Adam's lightning corner kicks that led to two goals for the Tangerines.

Then, in the second half, it all changes. Cool, classic Berbatov scores a first goal, then the little Mexican pea Chicharito, with his black gloves and predator disposition, drives a second one in. The Tangerines watch as their dream is snatched away, and now they know one more's coming, it's inevitable. The Bulgarian hit man does it again, scoring a third goal just two minutes from full-time. The arms rise up with that final whistle: Man United, undefeated and glorious. A loud chant ensues, and more blasphemy, the triumphant kind.

For a few minutes. Then it stops, there's no hanging around. The fans begin to trail down the steps into the night, the lights flicker off and the club is empty, silent as defeat. I think about the Blackpool fans leaving the stadium, but I know I'm the only one. The 'best team in the world' just won again and the loyal supporters have gone home to sleep, content and victorious in the generous bosoms of their wives.   *EM*

OUR LATE FANTASTICKS

Holly Knowles

A Cento

cĕn'tō, n. (pl.-os). Composition made up of scraps from other authors. [L,=patchwork garment]

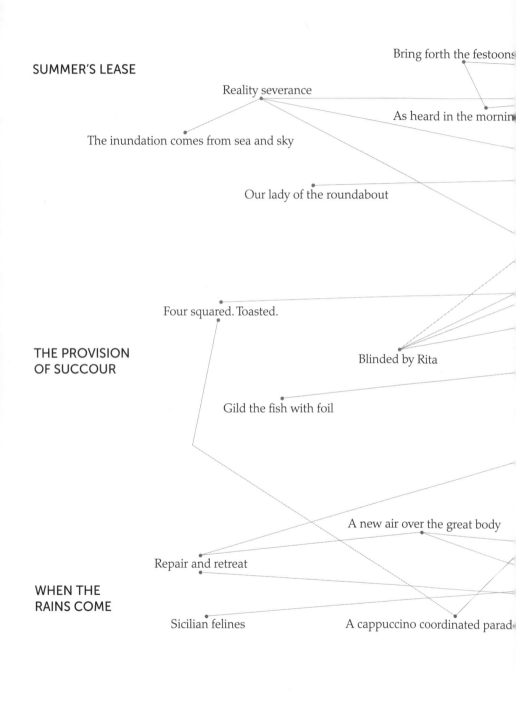

SUMMER'S LEASE

Bring forth the festoons

Reality severance

As heard in the mornin

The inundation comes from sea and sky

Our lady of the roundabout

Four squared. Toasted.

THE PROVISION
OF SUCCOUR

Blinded by Rita

Gild the fish with foil

A new air over the great body

Repair and retreat

WHEN THE
RAINS COME

Sicilian felines

A cappuccino coordinated parad

HUNTING
TOWERS
(2010)

Mark Mangion

Summer is best for migratory waders: Greenshank, Redshank, Spotted Redshank, Black-winged Stilt, Grey Plover, Ruff, Marsh, Curlew, Green, Wood and Common Sandpipers, Little and Teminck's Stints, and Dunlin. Other species include: Slender-billed Gull, Caspian Tern, White-winged Black Tern.

Winter Highlights: Little Grebe, Black-necked Grebe, Some ducks including Teal, Wigeon and Shelduck. Kingfisher, Moorhen, Water Rail, Chiffchaff, Robin, Moustached Warbler, Black Redstart, Stonechat, Song Thrush, White Wagtail, Water Pipit, Reed Bunting.

Autumn Highlights: Flamingo, Grey Heron, Night Heron , Little Egret, Marsh Harrier, Honey Buzzard, Osprey, Bluethroat, Red Breasted Flycatcher and other hirundines and passerines.

Spring Highlights: Waders: Little Ringed Plover, Ringed Plover, Common, Green, Wood Sandpipers, Ruff, Redshank, Little Stint and Dunlin. Grey and Purple Heron, Spoonbill, Swallows and Swifts. Passerines including Reed, Great Reed, Sedge, Wood, Willow, and Subalpine Warbler. Spotted, Collared and Pied Flycatchers.

KLABB
TAL-BOĊĊI

Tom Van Malderen

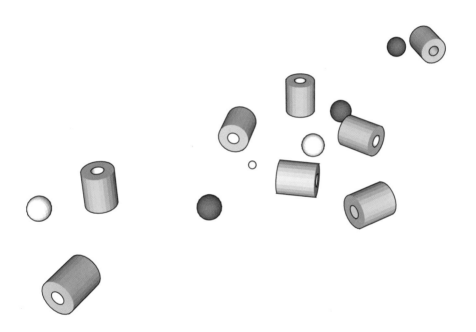

Boċċi is an old, traditional game closely related to French Pétanque, English bowls and the Italian Bocce. First records of the game in Malta trace back to the period of the knights of Saint John. Alongside the common spherical balls, Maltese Boċċi uses cylindrical ones that have the shape of a one-litre preserving can. The game has to be played by more than one player, requires great concentration and arms must be strong and not quivery.

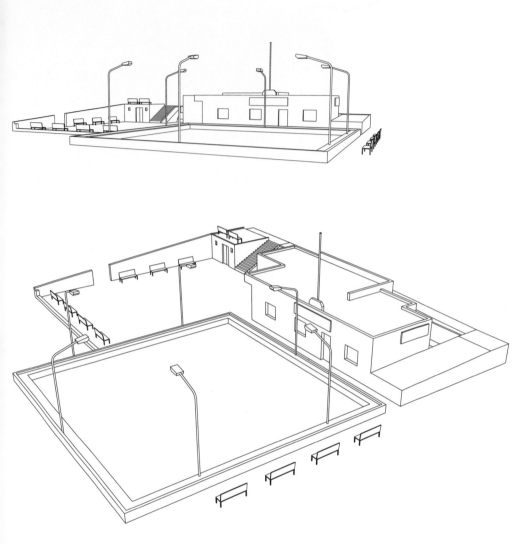

Klabb Tal-Boċċi, Floriana

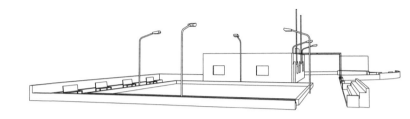

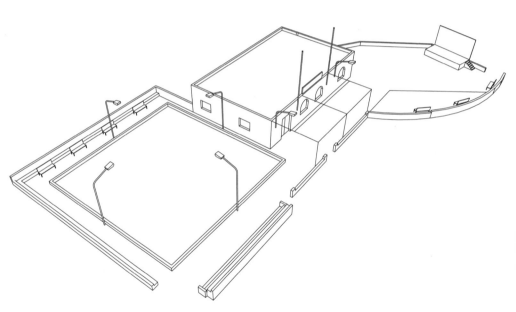

Klabb Tal-Boċċi, Pietà.

Most villages in Malta and Gozo have their own boċċi club. They are a hive of activity typically composed of 3 elements: a playground, a clubhouse, and an outdoor recreation ground that caters for events like bingo, the projection of football games and traditional Maltese Għana folk music.
Boċċi is played on a very smooth surface that is covered with coarse-grained sand. Today the game is under the control of a federation.
Official games are played between March and October, and mostly under artificial light.

REROUTE

DIVERSIONS, ITINERARIES & MINUTIAE

Route 01/
How To Find A Secret Beach Not Known as Skoll Ta' Barbaġanni

You will need to be on the island of Gozo, you will need a car, or a very generous local to take you there. Promise them watermelon and shade...
Also pack ice-cold Cisk and ħobż biż-żejt ftira sandwiches wrapped in tin foil.
Don't forget your lighter if you smoke.
Get in the car and follow signs to Qala, once you have found this village follow signs to Ħondoq.

You will know you are on the right track if you can see the islands of Malta and Comino to your right. The Gozo Channel ferry crosses frequently below.
Just before reaching the bottom of the hill, veer left onto a dirt track, You are not going to Ħondoq.
Sometimes, as dusk, two women can be seen seated at the side of the road as their goats graze. They smile, smile back.

Follow the road to a clearing and park.
To your right you will notice a shady area created by some eucalyptus trees, take shelter there and enjoy the view for a moment, you are about to walk in the scorching sun.

Head downwards and steer left. If you feel like you are trespassing walk faster.
You will notice a large, black board saying 'Cable' - this is a great beach, do not get too excited, this isn't where you are going.
You cannot see where you are going.
You are going to Secret Barn Owl Rock beach - this is not the official name of the beach. You will know it when you see it.
Undress and jump in.

Circumnavigate the rock with your mask and snorkel.
Emerge.
Head for the shade, slice watermelon, crack open a Cisk and pray you haven't lost your lighter.

Emma Mattei

178

Route 02/
Ħaġar Qim Swim

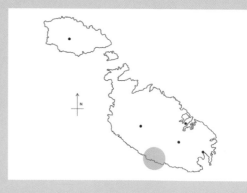

Ideally it is Summer. Take a bus, hitchhike, drive; it doesn't matter how you get to the megalithic temples of Ħaġar Qim and Mnajdra. Everyone knows how to guide you there. There's an entrance fee and an enormous canopy over the prehistoric stones. The magic temples of our lives have been trapped, some say protected. Entropy and the stones were working together just fine, but we are told of the need to preserve them for future generations.

We used to have picnics here when we were kids, but those days are long gone. And they were used as a backdrop for summer cultural festivals. But mostly it was hunters who walked around these structures; they weren't in awe of the stones in any way. So they blew it, and now the temples are surrounded and covered. So strange.

The temples - the oldest freestanding buildings in the world. Older than the pyramids! Go in and have a look. Arrive really early, say 9am, and maybe you'll get a moment alone.

If you get there and it's already too hot and too crowded, skip the visit for now, head to the entrance and then begin to walk around the fence, veering right, following the fence along. When you look out you'll see the island of Filfla. As a kid my father would tell us of the two-headed lizard found there.

David Attenborough went there with Desmond Morris to look for a subspecies of wall lizard, said to be endemic to the small, black island (hence its name, Filfla, reminiscent of a peppercorn).

Lacerta filfolensis is blackish with bluish spots. Attenborough found the Lacerta filfolensis, blackish with bluish spots, but not without putting them in danger with Morris catching the anchor of their boat on an unexploded mine.

Filfla was used as target practice by the British. It was considerably larger than it is today, with a freshwater spring, a chapel, a cave of wine and some sheep on it, should the fisherman find themselves stranded out at sea.

Nowadays Filfla is a nature reserve and out of bounds.

Walk towards Sir Walter Congreve's Memorial. He served as governor of Malta from 1924 to 1927, when he died. Romantically, he wished to be buried out at sea, between 'this spot and Filfla'; now the sea-passage is referred to as Congreve's Channel.

Walk carefully along the edge, scour the ground for black arrows. Keep your eyes peeled for a distant 'beach' painted on the rocks.

Don't give up, no matter how hot it is. Some shade and incredibly cool, clear waters wait for you below. The arrows always appear, eventually.

It is a gentle slope and a moderately easy walk down. Wear sensible shoes if you can. But it has been negotiated in flip flops too. Take some water, and sandwiches. The hotter you feel, the better the swim.

And take a mask and snorkel so you can swim through the archways into pebbled coves.

Reluctantly you will need to make your way up before sunset. Catch the last 15 minutes of visiting time at the temples, then have an icy cold Kinnie at the Ħaġar Qim Bar, in the cool of the outside terrace.

Emma Mattei & Juan Sarquis

Route 03/
The Walk Of The Secret Steps

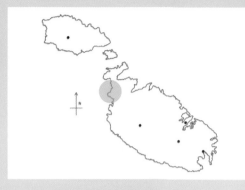

This walk is on rough terrain so be prepared, not necessarily walking boots – just the appropriate attitude will do. There are three approaches to this walk, here is one.

Approach the village of Manikata from the south and pass through. Invariably it will present you with something intriguing to look at. As you exit the village, you should pass the peach modernist edifice of Richard England's infamous coiled church, this is a big deal in architectural circles. You're aiming for the hill beyond this, so dip down into the valley and crawl up the other side.

As you near the crest of this hill look out for a driveable track on the left hand side. Take this track until you can sight a collapsing building about 200 metres from where you are. Park as you see fit – allow other cars to be able to pass and do not block even the faintest looking track if you want your tyres to be intact upon your return.

A few things about this walk:

It can be as long or as short as you want. If you expect a swim then allow 40 minutes to an hour before you hit the water.

In winter and spring the place is green with irreverent, hardy plants and flowers, in summer it is not.

'R.T.O', 'Privat', 'Private', mean don't walk on these bits.

There are paths, there are tracks between the paths – the type you see from above but not always whilst you are on them, choose accordingly, you are your guide.

Load up with the correct provisions, water, wine, picnic, depending on your constitution, and begin walking toward the collapsing building. Beyond there, head toward the cliff's edge. Once you reach the edge, head south looking for man-made steps descending down.

There is only one more landmark describable other than the many derelict farmer huts and hunter shacks. Along the cliff is a four-pillared, covered resting place, whose reasoning you will only notice whilst sheltering either from rain or sun. If you are here, then you will already have passed one set of steps 20 metres back along the cliff, there is another set 200 metres further south, choose one.

Having found a set of stairs pick a point of the coast below you wish to reach and descend, whilst doing so you may wish to marvel at their construction or the reasons for them.

Once you reach the bottom this guide ends. These tracks are not often walked, some vanish or are overgrown, some aren't, the discovery is all yours. Entry to the water is only truly easy at two points, there could be more, you'll see. Disappointment and wonder are reluctant bedfellows, below the cliffs you decide where you end.

Jon Banthorpe

Route 04/
The Blue Whole

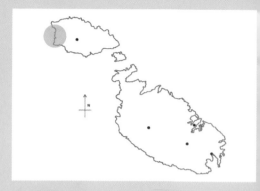

Jacques Cousteau found his legendary ship Calypso on these shores. The Inland Sea area in Gozo was allegedly a favourite diving spot.

We enter from the Blue Hole and turn left, swimming along the wall looking for a cave known as Coral Cave.

Along the way we see sponges and some spectacular tubeworms and fireworms. Do not touch these as the bristles break in your fingers and sting!

On this day there is an abundance of large grouper (ċerna). We find a couple of small caves, but they are not what we are looking for.

Eventually we find the Coral Cave at almost 30m depth, it has a large opening and a sandy bottom. The coral is False Coral[1], not valuable, but very fragile, so divers careful - do not to touch or accidentally hit it.

Our quest is over soon enough and it is time to surface.

Hannah Smith

---

1   *False coral (Myriapora truncata) Mediterranean Sea: This magnificent Bryozoan resembles the Red coral in colour and size, it is however much more fragile and loses its colour if removed from the sea. It is colonial, the minute pores and corresponding tentacles represent the individuals that make up the colony. Found in dimly lit areas from 2 to 90 metres depth.*

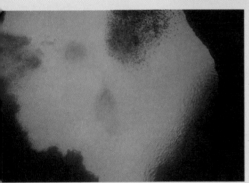

Route 05/
Instructions On How To Engage
With Baħrija

Head west to the town of Rabat and then follow signs to Baħrija, it's high and open out here. Once you have reached the village make your way down the main street until you reach a recreational garden and playing field. The road forks here, so take a right and follow the road along until it narrows. Simply park, or continue on your way if you've walked here from Rabat.

Overlooking the valley, notice a jungle of cane growing below. Beneath the cane runs a fresh water stream that is home to the endemic fresh water crab, called Qabru.

Cross the stream and walk up the pathway in between the fertile terraced fields until you see a vast view of the Mediterranean Sea.

Continue north along the spine of the hill, and pass through three gates. At the third gate dogs will appear. Be confident with the dogs.

Walk past the stone dwellings, built into the rock, and notice a newer house on the left side of the path. A hunter is active around the corner of the cliff.

To get a better view of Gozo, walk around this corner.

A bullet hits the rock above.

Sand and gravel drizzle down.

"Orrajt?" the hunter inquires from down below. Shout back "Just taking some pictures!" Take as many as you like, he might shrug.

Turn back and greet the people in the house of rock. "The hunter is from Awstralja," states one of them. "Awstralja - my onions," says the other.

The stone houses here were built by their forefathers, dating back four generations; the woman washes her hair in the spring water, before setting about preparing tea.

Since last year, sun panels on the roof provide electricity. Electricity, says the woman back with tea and lemons, has changed our life, from poor - to rich, clearly indicating low and high with her hand. Prior to the installation of the panels, the fridge was running on gasoline that produced unhealthy fumes. Now they have applied for a TV.

After finishing the delicious tea, take in the view one last time, then begin to walk back down the valley. If the sun has descended (and the Maltese sun sets rapidly) bear in mind the fresh water crab, and watch where you put your feet.

Erik Nordlander

Route 06/
Plane Of The Sea

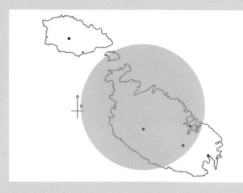

It is for some time that I have been thinking of getting a pilot's license. Not for commercial pursuits, just to gain enough experience to be able to fly to the edge of the Stockholm archipelago in a small plane. Living at times in Valletta by the Grand Harbour I watch the seaplane take off in the morning and in the afternoon, a De Havilland DHC3 Otter seaplane, number 406, one of a kind in Europe. My hand wants to control it, my intellect to leap inside. It becomes an expression of yearning and I succumb.

Instructions:
Walk down towards the Valletta Waterfront Terminal and purchase a scenic flight ticket for €80.
Recall references like The little Prince, Porco Rosso, Grizzly Man and Out of Africa...all mixed in with some winning National geographic documentaries with seaplanes landing on inaccessible mountain lakes.
Take a seat, feel the agility of the plane as it takes off, then watch how quickly you are elevated over the Grand Harbour.
This is like driving a car with no traffic; dramatic references are superfluous.
Press face to the window and identify the towns and villages and secret beaches that you might know.
Sit still for thirty minutes and enjoy landing on water.

Erik Nordlander

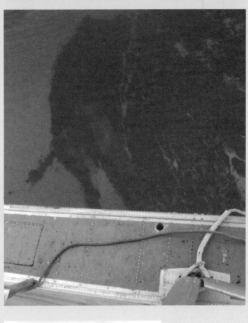

189

Route 07/
In Pursuit Of Ħobż Biż-Żejt

Bread with oil and tomatoes. A staple in the Maltese diet, occurring in varying degrees of oiliness, size and flair.

Purists take a slice of ħobż, rub a summer tomato on one side, add a drop of olive oil, sea salt and pepper. There are some who like the crusty end of the loaf, the qoxra, whilst others like a soft slice.

Here are the variations: we like to spread kunserva (rich tomato paste) onto the bread, which makes it sweet and salty. Then pile high with: chopped tomatoes, olives, vinegary capers, mint, sea salt and pepper. Additional ingredients include: finely diced onions or thinly sliced garlic (fresh, local), tinned tuna, ġardiniera, ġbejna, butter beans (fażola), parsley, lettuce, grated carrot.

Tastes exceptionally good after a long swim. Experts know to keep the tomato-olive-caper mix (taħlita) and bread separate. The mix goes into a jar, and if possible kept cool. Hold the slice in one hand and spoon the taħlita on, letting the juices trickle down your arm.

Most snack bars offer their own version: either between two slices, in an entire smaller version of the classic loaf, or in a hunk of unleavened ftira. Exceptional combos to be found at junctions, along industrial roads and in dock areas. Average price €1.50. Enjoy with cool Kinnie or bela té.

Marsa. Sammy's Bar. *This bar has been here since 1984. Two fresh slices of bread topped with meticulously chopped taħlita and tomato slices.*

Żebbug. Hunter's Bar. *Popular with hunters and heavyweights. This joint serves up all sorts of fast food, but we have always come here for the classic. Don't stray.*

San Ġwann. Mekkek Bar. *There are tables and chairs outside so you can watch the traffic as you snack, before continuing with the errands of the day.*

Birkirkara. Farfett Bar *is a hot spot for bargain ħobż biż-żejt. Don't say 'six bullets' when* sitting here.

St Paul's Bay. Johnny's Bar. *This bar has more of a pub feel to it, and stays open all hours. There's mint in the mix and the bread is exceptional.*

Valletta. Bonanno's Bar. *Situated opposite the old Customs House, table-talk at this bar has subsided since joining the EU, but the quality of fare is still the same. The landing stage of the gondola-like dgħajjes to take you across the harbour is situated just opposite.*

Julian Grech
Emma Mattei
Jon Banthorpe

Route 08/
Catch Him If You Can, The Bigilla Man

The Bigilla Van has been spotted in the following villages:
Tarxien
Vittoriosa
Kirkop
Siġġiewi
Qormi
Rabat

Features to look out for: Pre-recorded cry informing the neighbourhood that the best Bigilla is in town, possible cries include: Tal-Bigilla hawn! (the Bigilla man is here), Sħuna u Tajba il-Bigilla! (hot and delicious is our Bigilla); small van with horse silhouette motif; blue eyes; a lit 'Bigilla' sign that dangles inside the back of van (doors usually left open as van makes its way through town or village).

Essential ingredient: The dried Fava bean, known in Maltese as Ful tal-Ġirba.
Consistency: gloopy, warm.

Once located: Choose size of container: Start with the smallest one if you don't know what you're ordering. What you're ordering is a form of refried bean dish, with a kick.
The blue eyes light up. A metal lid is raised and a spoon immersed into the opening.
Bigilla is placed into the container.
You will be asked if you want felfel, this is chili to make it nice and spicy. He will also sprinkle fresh, chopped parsley on top.
Order a packet of galletti crackers to dip into the Bigilla.
Find a panoramic bench to sit on and dig in.
It's totally addictive, so, if the van hasn't driven off, run back for more.

Similarities: Mexican refried beans.
Rating: Two thumbs up from a Mexican.

Emma Mattei & Juan Sarquis

Route 09/
Folkitecture

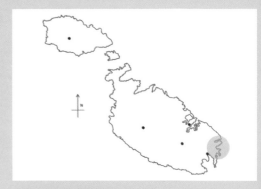

This is a walk for lovers of detail, of independence, for those who appreciate contrast.

Malta has a traditionally migratory population, though less so these days. But still, a large portion of inner city residents will vacate to beach houses and other sea related constructs for the summer months. These beach houses appear sporadically, most are illegal yet often older than legislation – meaning they remain. Some grow to form villages such as those in Valletta, Mellieħa, and St. Thomas' Bay. This is a closer look at the latter.

Get yourself to St. Thomas' Bay by bus (no. 30) or by car. Depending on the season of your visit the amount of people/sun will vary – no matter. Set back from the water's edge, beyond the boats and cafés (three), lie the summer houses. Built in indeterminate methods and times, each house is of its owner. Salvaged floor tiles become wall claddings, excess paint is re-used to give surprising combinations, and most boast novel responses to the need for furniture, shade, and boundaries.

The intimacy and personality of the summer homes and the density of their grouping could intimidate. You can explore – with respect. You may be invited in for tea, you may not. Concurrently, a camera can be a source of annoyance to some, it could be a source of entertainment to others.
You could communicate your interest, you may be told stories as reward. In any case, you lead the way.

Weather permitting, take a swim. Don't expect great fish dishes after, or even coffee to end your trip – this isn't that sort of place. Yet don't underestimate the satisfaction of salty tea and a plate of chips in the late afternoon.

                              Jon & Sandra Banthorpe

Insight 01/
Lights, Camera, Action

Luisa Bonello

Agora 2008 (St Michael's Ditch, Valletta)

Agora 2008 (the exterior of Alexandria at Marsaxlokk)

Agora 2008 (ancient Egypt in Fort Ricasoli, Kalkara)

Gladiator 1999 (Coliseum set at Fort Ricasoli in Kalkara)

The Devil's Double 2010 (Dominic Cooper on set)

The Devil's Double 2010 (Malta doubling for Iraq)

The Count of Monte Cristo 2002 (Comino)

Munich 2005 (on location in Bugibba)

Munich 2005 (St Paul's Street, Valletta)

Munich 2005 (Eric Bana and Geoffrey Rush in Sliema)

Troy 2003 (Blue Lagoon, Comino)

Insight 02/
What Tourists Are Supposed
To See

Bettina Hutschek

Salt Pans at Delimara Point (plus hunters)

Għar Dalam Museum

Grand Harbour

Sliema, especially the promenade

*Temple at Dolmen Hotel, Buġibba
- You can easily walk up to the
receptionist, ask to see the
Neolithic temple, and they will tell
you: "Yes, of course, just go down
this corridor, turn right into the
cafeteria, go into the court, pass
the swimming pool and you will
see it".*

Souvenir Shop, Rabat

Blue Grotto & the Great White catch

The Three Cities

Band Clubs

St. Paul's Cathedral, Mdina

Pastizzi Bakery, early morning hours

Opposite the Hypogeum in Paola

Mellieħa with beautiful views...

Valletta Steps

Gozo Ferry

... & Mellieħa Bay

Republic Street & Fountains

Triton Fountain

St. Paul's Bay

Scenery

Saints & Processions

Cart Ruts

Temples in Mnajdra & Ħaġar Qim

Marsaxlokk

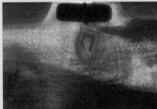
Citadel, Victoria, Gozo

St. Julian's

Dingli Cliffs

A City Itinerary/
Valletta & Floriana
"The Splendid Town Quite like a Dream"

Valletta is Europe's bijou capital, Floriana her protective suburb. There is great rivalry between the two, complementary yet distinct in their differences; Valletta, civitas humilissima, is a baroque paean with mannerist flourishes and hurried post-war construction, Floriana, much of which had to be rebuilt after the war, offers open spaces, a large granary, a football pitch, two enormous hotels and a maze of public gardens.

The fortified city and its environs swell to full capacity with the daily workforce, then shrink back after hours, when the residents reclaim the streets; with a population of around 6,000 in Valletta, and with only 2,600 in Floriana, night is an intimate affair.

There are particular rhythms and seasonal trends; the city is at its busiest in the mornings, remaining vibrant over lunch, and then dozing in the early afternoon. This is a good time to seek out the Turner and Lear at the National Museum of Fine Arts, or gawp at Caravaggio's brutal beheading at St. John's co Cathedral. Murder, however, is not always digestible, and some might prefer to doze in a shady public garden, or head down to the rocks and dip their feet in the sea.

Afternoons are more leisurely. Shops reopen at 4pm, then three hours later the shop fronts close up and the streets empty out. An evening melancholy fills the air but don't be disheartened, have an aperitif and wait for the restaurants to open for dinner, alternatively seek out a bolt hole bar or band club and get local. Some evenings there are plays and concerts at the Manoel Theatre, St. James Cavalier centre for creativity and the MITP, whilst the Embassy cinema has daily showings. Saturday shopping is half day and Sunday is most definitely the day of rest. Summer is the quietest season for capital when many offices work reduced hours.

Stay in Valletta and Floriana a while, experience the ebb and flow of the capital on the peninsula. For luxury art deco, echoes of heads of state, magical gardens, fine dining and a colonial Club Bar with perfect gin & tonics check into the Phoenicia Hotel. If your budget is less flexible, head towards Battery street, to the British Hotel; here Maltese artist Emvin Cremona's work can be seen in the wrought iron balconies and balustrades. The lobby and the bar remain intact, an absolute must for retro aficionados; it's also a good place to sample braġjoli and rabbit and take in the view of the harbour. There are also numerous studios and apartments available to rent on a daily basis: Valletta Studios, G-House, 51 Battery Street and Maison La Vallette.

Shop, drop in, pop open a bottle, let's eat. Republic Street is the main thoroughfare, jewellers, purveyors of fine wines and perfumes, mobile phone shops, boutiques, opticians and the archaeological museum, all vying for your attention; walk along until you reach Palace Square then continue to Casa Rocca Piccola, an ancestral family home open to the public. R. Grech Jewellers at Nos. 69-70 specialise in Gran Spinat and filigree.

The side streets offer a more discerning flavour of old. So attempt zigzagging through the streets.

Start your day with a cappuccino and pastizz at Caffé Cordina (244, Republic street). If you're in a hurry, stand at the counter, drink an espresso and order a croissant; you may have to elbow your way in to stand amongst the smart lawyers in their fine Italian shoes. Marvel at the ceiling and other elaborate fittings. Step into Republic Square and greet the British Queen Victoria who can proudly wave again, having recently got all her fingers back.

Old Treasury Street

A small shop under the arches, FotoVision stocks Leica cameras, including vintage stock for collectors. Further along is Tikka Bar, return here before lunch for an aperitif of Campari orange and some amuses bouches, or ħniżrijiet as we call them, courtesy of the proprietor.

Merchant Street

The morning market on Merchant Street is densely packed with hawkers selling bras, g-strings, wallets, t-shirts, fabric and so on. This market is dictated by price: you can get anything you want for under €10. The challenge is to weave amongst the stalls from one side of the street to the other, until you emerge.

The Main Tourist office is located at the top of this street, a good place to pick up a map and find out if there's anything special going on in

Statue of St Paul in Republic Street.

town. On Monday and Wednesday mornings, between 9 - 11am there is a bazaar upstairs at the Faith, Hope & Charity Uffiċju Missjunarju, where thrift addicts can pick up vintage.. N.Caruana House Furnisher is an emporium of appliances and utensils.

The Electro Store has bulbs and adaptors aplenty. At no. 14, you will find an Mdina Glass outlet, pick up a piece in the classic Blue Roman or Blue Crysal. Camilleri Paris Mode stocks garment and wedding gown fabrics, offers a dress making service, and stocks luxury items such as Acqua di Parma and Dr. Vranjes. Antiques and Fine Arts at no. 31, proffer porcelain for the avid collector: Meissen, Dresden and Sitzendorfer to name a few. Albion Stores at no. 201 is where serious cake makers go, figolli cutters can be found here. G. Xuereb is where one can order made-to-measure trousers, but be sure to make an appointment as the tailor only pops in once a week, on Monday between 9.30am - 11am. The mecca for suits is Bortex at nos.54-55, whilst Francis Bajada Menswear at no. 192, is where the well-heeled chaps go to stock up on their finery, and in summer, one can pick up a genuine Panama hat made in Ecuador.

St Paul's Street.
The best time of year to visit is on the 10th February during the feast of St Paul's Shipwreck, the first and the finest in the church almanac. Devotion is intense and nationwide, a link to the past when Valletta had over 50,000 residents.
The rest of the year one can pop into bazaars and general stores that continue to tick over quietly. Purchase tea and honey at L-Arka fair trade shop, clean up your back and sides at Freddie the Barber (open till midday), then find the pink restaurant, Ristorante San Paolo where you can enjoy a dozen and a half of the best-ever ricotta ravioli.

St. Christopher Street.
Il-Ħorża is a tiny restaurant with big flavour. Perfect for a romantic dinner for two. There's a Tal-Lira clock-maker a few doors up, stick your head around the door and say hello.

Archbishop Street.
Savour chef Christopher's menu at his restaurant Ambrosia located at No. 137. The blackboard tells you what's on the menu that day. Favourites include goat-cheese soufflé, lampuki goujons and pannacotta; a mecca for all gourmands. The Pub next door is where we raise our pint glasses to actor Oliver Reed and his last drink. There are tales of 'strange appearances' in photographs taken there.

Old Theatre Street.
For fine loose leaf tea by weight pop into Café Palazz. This is also a good place to pick up some kannolli made daily with fresh ricotta. Marks & Spencer is Malta's most established British department store; located on four storeys this is where we go to get our essentials, from beach towels to French wine. Manoel Theatre is on this street so pop in to see what's showing. Walk towards the Anglican Pro Cathedral and read the plaque on the corner of West Street, commemorating Sir Walter Scott's visit in 1931. Of Valletta it was he who said: a splendid town quite like a dream. He stayed here at the Beverly Hotel 'into which the Palazzo Britto had been converted'.
Head back up the street, beneath the theatre is Fumia, serving fresh fish and shellfish with Sicilian flair (the street entrance is on Old Bakery Street). Cordial restaurant referred to as Chez Cyrille serves up authentic foie, moules and crepes suzette.

St. Lucy Street.
Pick up an antique gold item on the stretch between Republic Street and Merchant Street. Valentino Belgian chocolates are delicious, try the one filled with caramel and salt. Grab a bite and have a perfect cup of coffee at Piadina Caffé, any time from mid-morning. Legligin is where to go in the evenings for a good bottle of wine and delicious tapas. Return to this street at 4am for piping hot pastizzi served at the bakery, you'll see it when the white door is open and the light is on.

St. John's Street.
L-Ingliż Caffé is always welcoming and always open, a good place to hob-nob. The haberdashery is a dream of trims and sequins - just pretend you know how to sew and enter. Croce Bonaci is a popular pit-stop for a coffee and cake.

Zachary Street.
Capri caffé on the corner serves up a quick fresh orange juice for €2, whilst further on Valletta residents pick up their fruit and vegetables. Discretely tucked away is Edwards, Lowell stockists of Rolex, Philippe Patek and Vertu phones. Head to Gambrinus for a time-warp coffee break.

Melita Street.
Just step into Pisani Electrical Store and pretend you need something, take home a 'flickering' flame bulb, or one with a Christmas tree filament inside. Blush and Panic boutique is a vintage and retro-inspired treasure trove of clothes, books, accessories and whimsy. If

Newspapers, Merchant Street

you get a lunchtime table at **Da Pippo's** *lucky you! This is the Valletta trattoria par excellence and serves delicious pasta in padella with plenty of gusto and charm.* **Upim** *is an Italian department store if you need filo di scozia socks or a monochrome, purple umbrella.* **Museum Caffé** *is an institution, take a seat.*

South Street.
Prego *cafeteria at No. 58 serves a mighty egg sandwich and offers cool, calm respite in a capsule of mid-sixties décor.* **Merisi** *opposite does great coffee.* **Maestro's** *latest incarnation as bistro has proved very popular.* **The Carriage** *is a stalwart of fine dining in Valletta, occupying a terrace that overlooks Marsamxett.*

Strait Street.
Trabuxu *is an intimate wine bar and popular hang out spot that is always busy, serving platters even after the theatre show is over.* **Frascati** *is the lawyers' hideaway daytime bar. The invisible man* **Buġelli** *opens his warehouse between 10-12.30 to sell books.*

Sunny days, Summer nights.
Eating outdoors is not as easy as you might think in Valletta. **Malata** *on Palace Square is family-run and always an authentic affair.* **Sicilia Bar** *at No.1 on St John's Street occupies a patio soaked in winter sun and serves up great pasta marinara and al faruk. Just below is the* **Bridge Bar** *where George puts cushions on the steps and is very popular on Friday with its live jazz nights. The* **Gun Post** *on the city peripheral road is a wonderful spot and the* **QEII** *just outside the Lower Barrakka Gardens is perfect for summer night beers.*

The Public Gardens
In summer there is cool shade, in winter there is sun. Some gardens are very public and seen from afar, others are discrete, revealing their beauty only to those who enter. Several are well known to the locals, others less so. Some are usurped by the views; others have limited visiting hours and exotic cacti.

Enter **The Palace** (Il-Palazz) *from Republic Square into* **Prince Alfred's** *courtyard and you will see jacaranda mimosifolia, nerium oleander, hibiscus and palms with lovely names like kentia elegantissima and Chamaerops humilis.*

In the larger courtyard notice bronze Neptune, salvaged from the fish market (pixxkerija) by British Governor Le Marchant in the 19th century. Once, there were oranges here (Republic Square was an orangery until 1897). Now it is paved to receive heads of state in black vehicles.

The fortifications, which measure roughly 3 kilometres, are comprised of 30 bastions in which gardens have taken shape over the centuries. Make your way towards **Castille** *and the* **Upper Barrakka Garden**, *known as Il-Barrakka ta' Fuq. The garden stands on what was called the bastion of St Peter and St Paul; it is a very popular meeting place and wedding reception venue because of the spectacular vista over the harbour. At midday a canon is blasted over the harbour, it's deafening. One can now head down to the* **Lower Barrakka Garden** *(Il-Barrakka t'Isfel), praying it is September to catch a glimpse of the hanging Kigelia Africana. It is from here that we can imagine the Maltese people watching the warships sail into harbour past the breakwater. These days, enormous cruise liners roll in each morning. No one goes to watch them.*

Hastings Garden *in the Spring you is a plethora of flowering trees, and if you are there in autumn look out for the Tulip tree which turns bright red. Walk to the end and look down over Marsamxett creek.*

Leave Valletta and head to Floriana that has more gardens: **Kalkara Garden**, **Sir Luigi Preziosi Garden**, *the* **Garden of Repose** *(formerly a cemetery), the secret* **Sa Maison Garden** *which is ideal for lunchtime love trysts and the extra special* **Argotti Botanic Gardens**, *known as Il-Gotti. It is the commonwealth's third oldest botanical garden and there are over 200 specimens of cacti and succulents.*

Outside Argotti you will see one of Grand Master Wignacourt's aqueduct towers. Search for the entrance to **St. Philip Garden** *and enter through the gate, descend the ramp and pass through the tunnel. There you will find a massive gate that can swing up by chains. Now you are faced with two flights of steps leading upwards, run up and there, in perfect symmetry, are eight cypress trees, around the three-tiered fountain, where mythical dolphins slowly disintegrate beneath giant scallops. Inaugurated in 1615 by Grand Master Wignacourt in St George's Square in Valletta, the British moved it here to make space for military parades. It is wistful, exquisite and lonely,*

Step away from the ancient fountain towards the vantage point above Portes des Bombes, known as Bombi, the grand entrance to Floriana. Below imagine the now defunct train travelling towards Valletta from Mdina.

Gaze out past the dockyard cranes; scan towards the Southern coastline, then inland to the higher ground. You are a sentinel atop the military walls, and it is time to exit the city referred to by Walter Scott as 'quite like a dream'.

Emma Mattei & Jon Banthorpe

Lower Barrakka Gardens

A Contrary Itinerary/
Gozo
Insulaphilia

Growing up in the seventies in Malta was frugal. There was very little money in our parents' pockets, and not much for sale in the shops. The idea of a family holiday, which most kids demand today, was somewhat of a dream. We were the holiday destination, and the furthest we would go was Gozo, the island 25 minutes away by ferry.

Each summer we would head out there, set up camp at Uncle Joe's house or in a 'holiday flat', and spend the days and nights outdoors, creating a stockpile of over-bright memories; sandcastle red of Calypso's beach and snorkelling blue of Għar Qawqla in Marsalforn. Despite the proximity, that 'holiday feeling' was understood. The ferry ride was most symbolic, with mum and dad kicking back on deck, that wind, that sun... time trickled by so slowly, with swimming as the main activity of the day, everyone always so tanned, taking long afternoon naps and preparing lackadaisical suppers. Best of all, we got to stay up late and sit by the sea with friends.

The years roll by, but I still follow that itinerary when I am here. It is a place to be carefree, languid, aquatically active, or motionless on the scorching rocks. Ideally first experienced at the height of summer, 'that holiday feeling' will call you back time and time again.

Summer here requires flip-flops, a good novel and a hammock. Winter calls for stoic silence, acceptance, a waterproof jacket for long walks and a desire for melancholia.

Here is contrary itinerary compiled with my friend Emma Winter who returns to Gozo each year to unwind from danger! high voltage! life in Paris. We recommend renting a car, and booking a place to spend the night before you arrive.

Firstly, some notes on the importance of

contrariness. Often people say: I spent the day 'on' Gozo: I think they do that because it is a small island. But no one should say that about any place – it implies some sort of gargantuan stride atop a miniscule heap, a resident of Brobdingnag treading carelessly.

Often they are day-trippers. Rising early, they pack a ham-n-cheese sandwich and jump on a bus. They arrive at Ċirkewwa harbour, dazed, suitable sandals already slipping on the hot asphalt. At 9am they board the ferry and order a cup of coffee, looking towards Comino in the blinding sun.

I imagine the 9-5 tour: a walk around the old citadel, expressions of amazement at the majesty of the Ġgantija temples, and a holiday snapshot down at the Azure Window in Dwejra where that scene from Clash of the Titans was shot. I imagine it to be a hot, rushed day that sees them back in Mġarr Harbour to catch the 5pm ferry.
So turn the itinerary on its head. Catch the ferry to Gozo at 5pm and plan to stay there until midnight the next day.

The ferry takes 25 minutes. It is not long enough. Always make your way to the top deck. You will cruise past Comino and come into Mġarr harbour, where many cars will be lined up to catch the ferry you are arriving on. Suggestions on how to wind down into Gozo 'island-stood-still' mode:

Always stop at **Gleneagles** on the way up the hill to initiate the vacation. Superb gin & tonics and Pimms no. 1 cocktails served here. On the terrace we love to watch the horses cooling down in the harbour below.

An early evening swim at Ramla L-Ħamra, Calypso's beach where Ulysses came to shore and was the subsequently stranded for seven years. A look at the valley in the early evening might explain why.
Evening shower at your farmhouse or holiday flat (doesn't really matter where you stay as you'll be out and about all the time, most fun would be to stay in a trullo-style detached bungalow at **Ta' Ċenċ Hotel**, and let the marvellous cricket morning song wake you up!).

Head back down to the harbour and dine at a restaurant filled with families and friends (all tanned). Kids behave better when parents are not stressed by the daily grind. **Bella Sicilia** and Sammy's **Kċina Tal-Barrakka** are both good.

Then make your way up to **Żeppi's Pub** in Qala

Gleneagles Bar, Gozo

and have a drink with Alex and Sonia. Stay there as long as you can, then drive towards the lighthouse in Żebbug to see the lights in Sicily.

Rise at dawn, watch first light creep across the silent skies. Reach out for your copy of Homer and spellbound, read: When Dawn spread out her fingertips of rose....

If it is summer head to the nearest rocks for an early morning swim, brew coffee beforehand and take it with you in a flask. This should be done before 9am for maximum sensation.
If it is winter, brew coffee and open the windows or walk outside into the street, or onto the balcony, or out into the garden, and let the fresh air wake you.

Make your way to the **Coney Island Bar** in Victoria for breakfast. Georgia will make you tea in a glass, with lemon, or milky with loads of sugar; to eat order two pastizzi, "wieħed irkotta, wieħed piżelli" and buy a copy of The Times of Malta. Sit at one of the formica tables and scan the headlines as President Kennedy smiles down at you.
Mid morning and the capital is bustling. Fisherman hats, vegetables, beach towels and Chinese plimsolls can all be bought here at the It-Tokk market.
A good detour is the **Maritime Museum** in Nadur, where flotsam and jetsam from our lives aquatic can be viewed.

The day ahead of you offers a variety of beaches to choose from. Always check which way the wind is blowing to ensure clean waters.

The 'brain cave' at **Fungus Rock**, has deep, cool waters and the chance to sit inside the earth, it is here that you can make a wish.

Għar Qawqla is the rocky cove in Marsalforn that somehow never gets crowded, it offers a great jumping-off rock for daredevils and a natural jacuzzi.
Take ħobż biż-żejt with you for lunch, but if you decide to leave try **Gesther's** in Xagħra for traditional home cooking. Don't arrive any later than 12:30. The incredible Ġgantija temples are just around the corner.

For the ultimate fishfeast by the sea, head to Mġarr Ix-Xini, a fjord-like inlet where the freshest fish is cooked outdoors with the simplest of ingredients. A bottle of white wine goes down well in the shade of the Tamarisk trees.

Always head home for a nap. En route take a meditative moment – walking into an ornate, cool church and then walking out from the gilted, fan-driven inner, back into the light, through a red cloth that hangs down behind the brown, heavy door.

Afternoon swimming: Head to **San Blas** (very steep descent). Enjoy the long shadows on the sand as the sun begins to set.

Other good swimming spots: **Hondoq, Kantra, Xatt L-Aħmar**
Evening activities: Head to the Senap Cliffs for a spectacular Mediterranean vista.
Cool off at **Fontana**, where fresh water from a spring situated in the Kerċem valley nearby runs into stone basins under the arch. This is a perfect pit stop to rinse the salt off your skin, and much more fun than heading home.

Sundowners on the terrace outside the **Saint Patrick's Hotel**, perfect for people watching and chatting.

Tapies in Victoria is always a good halfway house between beach and home or home and dinner.

Night swimming, at the height of summer, is easily done along the accessible shore.
Always head back to **Gleneagles**, linger there as long as you can and catch the midnight ferry back.

Emma Mattei & Emma Winter

San Lawrenz, Gozo

Għar Qawqla, Gozo

Stolen Notes From Little Black Books

Where to shop:

Furnishings & Books: Ċeramika Maltija at Villa Bologna, St. Anthony Street, Attard, for artisan pineapple lamp bases, artichoke bowls, horse heads and Queen Elizabeth busts. The Pottery traces its roots back to the 1920s.

Island Books in Mosta, open only at weekends, for rare Melitensia and obscure literary finds.

Mdina Glass, Ta' Qali Crafts Village, Blue crysal is collectible. Mdina Glass has been in production since the early seventies.

Food/drink:

Busy Bee, Msida for ricotta kannoli, ottijiet for dipping into tea and almond biscuits. This institution was established in 1933.

Antica Pasticceria Siciliana, Nazzarenu Street, Sliema, for everything sweet in mini and maxi versions.

The White Sheep on rue D'Argens, Gżira, a delicatessen with both local and imported goods, also serves delicious sandwiches.

Maneri's along the Gżira Strand for fresh Sicilian cheeses, salami, olive oil and wine, including the zibibbo variety.

Ice cream and affogato at Dolci Peccati on Tower Road.

Try:

Kinnie a citrusy soft drink, Twistees a cheesy snack in a packet, Cisk the local beer (lager, Hopleaf, Blue Label),

Pick up:

(Perishable) Ilma żaħar (orange blossom water), for cooking or as a tonic for skin; fennel seeds for roast potatoes the Maltese way; olive oil; carob syrup, used in cooking and as a substitute for cough medicine; sea salt; capers in vinegar, the smaller the bud the better; olives (we like them bitter); kunserva, tomato concentrate that makes everything taste sweet and delicious. Lejla carob liqueur produced by Meridiana Wine Estate.

(Permament) Antique gold chains and charms; antique lace; antique silver coffee pot; filigree; replica 'coin ashtrays'; a ġewlaq (soft basket); a cane blind for your windows; local tiles still manufactured in San Gwann; antique, sheep wool carpets (rare); brass doorknockers; fisherman hats. L-Arloġġ Tal-Lira, a wall clock consisting of a gilded wooden case and dials adorned with picturesque scenes(you'll have to ship this one home). Ganutell, artificial flowers made from wire, thread and beads.

Markets:

Fruit, vegetables, flowers, fish, plants, pots, pans, plimsolls and other paraphernalia. Most markets are mornings only unless specified. Sunday markets do linger on a little longer. Early is always best, beat the heat and the crowds. Here is a list of some of the markets and the days on which they happen.

Daily:

Merchant Street, Valletta (the fresh produce is located inside the building adjacent to it known as Is-Suq) plenty of tea towels and t-shirts found here, It-Tokk, in Victoria, Gozo, offers a good blend of traditional and new. (Merchant Street market is closed on Sundays).

Markets:

Monday Mosta.

Tuesday Cospicua, Ta' Qali farmers' market (afternoons).

Wednesday Birkirkara.

Thursday Żurrieq, Birżebbuġa.

Friday Paola, Żebbuġ.

Saturday Qormi. Ta' Qali farmers' market (mornings).

Sunday Antiques Flea market in Birgu. Marsaxlokk fish market (look out for the small jars of garlic-chilli paste at the 'spice lady' stand).

Some markets listed above may be open on additional days to those specified.   EM

Flea Market

CONTRIBUTORS

Andrew Alamango is a cultural marauder, musicologist, producer, musician and cook. He has been instrumental in raising social awareness of Maltese folk and popular music. Recent productions include the Etnika Project and Malta's Lost Voices.

Geoffrey Aquilina Ross is an author, editor and columnist; during the sixties he was the first male fashion editor with British Vogue. His first book was an amusing study, How to Survive the Male Menopause, and since then he has written and edited a number of travel guides and fine photography books. His memoir of fashion in sixties London, The Day of the Peacock, was published by the Victoria & Albert Museum, London (2011).

Kurt Arrigo is amphibious. He has always been captivated by the sea, above and below the surface. His first solo book, Malta: A Coastal Journey, was published in 2005. As a Rolex photographer, he travels extensively, but always enjoys returning home to his family.

Sandra Banthorpe is part Maltese, part English, part Dutch, part artist, part collector. She currently resides in Malta, pretending it's actually the wild, wild west.

Chris Bianchi was born in Malta in 1977. He attended Middlesex University and the Royal College of Art. He has worked for a range of magazines, publishers, record labels, and leading fashion brands. He is also an animator and has worked on music videos, for the likes of Dirty Stop Outs, Kissy Sell Out, and The Plugs, as well as for various film festivals. When not at the drawing table, Chris works on a musical project called Nairobi Lovers and produces a quarterly newspaper publication called Bare Bones. He is a founder member of LE GUN magazine - a publication that explores the narrative side of illustration and storytelling.

Elise Billiard holds a Ph.D. in anthropology; she is currently a visiting lecturer on Material Culture at the University of Malta (Department of Anthropology). But this is just a cover; in reality she is a professional tourist. Some years ago she attended the École des Beaux Arts in Marseille and pretended to be an artist by exhibiting in several European countries.

Luisa Bonello was involved in the Malta Film Commission since its inception in 1999. Of course, what she really wants to do is act...

studied archaeology at York University, but is gainfully employed in the production of water biscuits and other baked goods. His petrolhead credentials are limited to watching his brother race and restoring a 1967 Alfa Romeo. **Joshua de Giorgio**

is the author of The International Dictionary of Artists who Painted Malta. He has made considerable contributions to art and history publications, and was curator of a Grade 1 historic house in Gloucestershire, in England. He returned to his native Malta with his English wife and four children to settle in Valletta, where he has restored and opened Casa Rocca Piccola, a patrician Maltese House and Costume Museum. He is a founder member of Fondazzjoni Patrimonju Malti, a member of the Committee of Privileges of the Maltese Nobility, Rector of the Archconfraternity of the Most Holy Rosary and a Council member of the Maltese Association of the Order of Malta. **Nicholas de Piro**

is a history graduate who has researched and published extensively on 18th century Malta. He is also a keen researcher about food in Early Modern Malta He is currently the curator of the Malta Maritime Museum. **Liam Gauci**

was born in Malta and lives in London. She is interested in history, memory and nostalgia in relation to a sense of place. Making use of photography, drawing and writing, she attempts to capture the memories and forgotten anecdotes found in architecture. **Nina Gerada**

is from Scotland but lives and works in London. He plans to return to Malta to perfect his pierogi. **Andrew Gow**

spends as much time as possible swimming and diving. **Julian Grech**

was born in Malta and educated in Switzerland, England and Italy, where he lives and works. He is a freelance product designer working in Italy and worldwide. An ardent lover of the arts, he spends much of his leisure time travelling between Milan, Paris, Noto and Senglea. He has strong ties to his Maltese origins and his beloved home in the Grand Harbour. **Gordon Guillaumier**

is a visual artist who uses everyday observations to tell stories in video and performance work. She has studied and worked in Florence, Augsburg, Berlin, Barcelona, Leipzig, Brest, New York, Bucharest and Malta. She currently lives in Berlin where she reads Borges and eats dark chocolate. **Bettina Hutschek**

grew up on the Isle of Man. She swapped one tiny isle for another and has been living in Malta for five years. She works from her Valletta refuge as a journalist, enjoying flea markets, summer and Twistees. **Holly Knowles**

is from Kluczbork in southwest Poland. An interior architect based in Valletta, she looks at the sea first thing in the morning, **Wioletta Kulewska** whilst at night she is happiest with a dish of pierogi and a glass of wine. Wioletta wishes she were born before the car occupied the street.

Harry Malt lives and works in the East London Dream Zone. He produces Bare Bones, a quarterly art paper funded by its creators. He collects hen's teeth and is available for all commissions.

James Manduca lives in Mdina. He is a recently graduated architect.

Mark Mangion is a visual artist and independent curator based in Paris and Valletta. He is the founder and director of Malta Contemporary Art.

Sacha Maric lives in Copenhagen with his wife and daughter. He takes pictures for a living and thinks he's lucky that his hobby is also his job. He likes the Danish way of life, riding his bike around and eating pickled fish on rye bread. He was born and raised in London.

Erik Nordlander prefers to dream by day and look sharp by night. He first visited Malta in 2005 to work as a table tennis coach. He currently lives in Lund, Sweden.

David Pisani is a professional photographer, specialising in architecture and design. He has worked on numerous architectural and conservation projects including commissions by the Government of Malta, the UNESCO World Heritage Committee, the Getty Foundation and the Courtauld Institute. He has lectured at the University of Malta's Faculty of Architecture on photography and conservation technology. He is the founder and director of SITEWORK, an architectural workshop for children.

Edward Said likes bikes, boats, films and sea, and now rocks. He is a filmmaker and casting director.

Juan Sarquis lives in Mexico City. In 2008 he set up Filmaciones de la Ciudad. His recent production, Esperandos a Los Bitles, is a film about a Mexican Beatles tribute band that travels to Liverpool.

Hannah Smith has been diving since she was old enough to get a license without her mother's permission. Whilst working on cruise liners, she got the opportunity to dive many different sites around the world, but her favourite will always be the inland sea and the blue hole in Gozo.

Nick Tabone was born and raised in Canada. He spends most of his time on tallships, and likes to return to Malta whenever he can.

Amelia Troubridge lives in London with her husband and son. Working as a photographer for 15 years, Amelia has shot for TIME magazine, Vanity Fair, Vogue, Harpers Bazaar, Condé Nast Traveller, Tatler and The Saturday and Sunday Times Magazine. She has published two solo books and has had her work auctioned and exhibited at Phillips de Pury, Christie's and The ICP in NY.

swapped Belgium for Malta, where he works as an architect. **Tom Van Malderen**
He occupies a flat in Valletta with his growing collection of
timeworn lamps. Whilst dealing with the ambiguity of his
profession, he prefers a simple life, testing configurations of
space.

is Professor of English Literature at the University of Malta, **Peter Vassallo**
where he was formerly Head of the English Department. He
holds the degrees of MA and D.Phil from the University of
Oxford. He has specialized in British Romantic Literature and
is an internationally recognized authority on Lord Byron. He
was President of the International Association of University
Professors of English (IAUPE).

is a political journalist and satirical columnist with newspaper **Raphael Vassallo**
Malta Today. Born in Sliema in 1971, he studied English and
theatre at the University of Malta and obtained a Masters
degree in journalism from the University of Cardiff in 2006.
He is a campaigner for secular issues and in 2010 co-founded
the Malta Humanist Association. He currently lives in Ta' Xbiex
with a neurotic, calico cat named Maggie.

is a walker and a writer by vocation, a translator by profession. **Alex Vella Gera**
He hopes one day to discover the Malta beyond those thick,
white clouds on the horizon, which he swears are really
mountains.

lives in a fin de siècle fantasy world of the mysterious unknown; **Steph von Reiswitz**
murder, alchemy, genteel hedonism and civilised depravity.
She works as an artist and illustrator in London.

is a German artist. She appreciates the nineties dance floor **Franziska von Stenglin**
music still played on the radio in Malta, and the delicious
pastizzi and tea served in the hunter's bar in Rabat.

was born in Belgrade in 1971. He is the founder of Kinemastik **Slavko Vukanovic**
and director of the Kinemastik International Short Film Festival.

currently lives and works in Paris where she presides as studio **Emma Winter**
director for the handbags at Louis Vuitton. Gozo is her antidote.

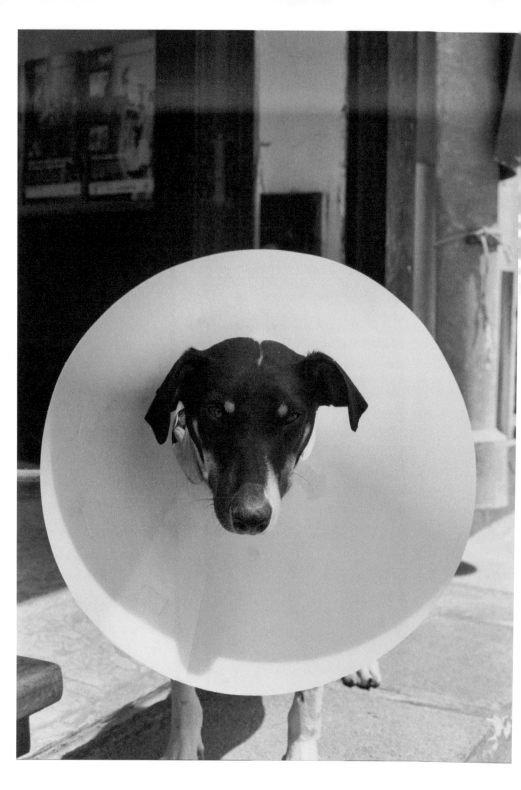

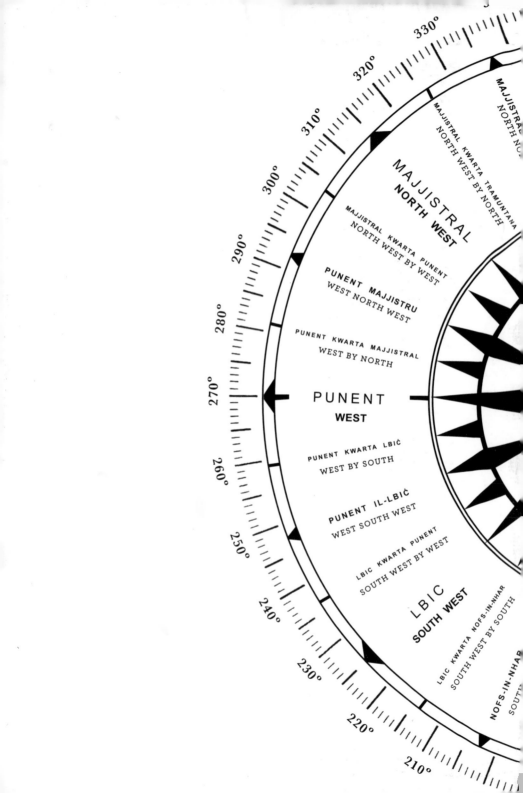